A SHORT
HISTORY
OF
SCOTLAND

RICHARD KILLEEN

GILL & MACMILLAN

DEDICATION

To
DRK
with admiration and gratitude

TEXT: Richard Killeen
EDITOR: Fleur Robertson
DESIGN: Triggerfish, Brighton
Production: Karen Staff, Neil Randles

Published in Ireland
by Gill & Macmillan Ltd
Hume Avenue, Park West, Dublin 12
with associated companies
throughout the world.
www.gillmacmillan.ie

CLB 4994
Originally published by
Quadrillion Publishing Ltd.
© Salamander Books Ltd., 2001, 2004

An imprint of **Chrysalis** Books Group plc

ISBN 0 7171 2645 5
Printed in China

CONTENTS

INTRODUCTION

This short history is an attempt to survey the Scottish past in a manner that is at once dispassionate and comprehensive. It assumes no previous knowledge on the part of the reader.

The uniqueness of the Scots has been acknowledged at least since early medieval times. Their status as a separate nation has not been in doubt since the 14th century. As I hope the text makes clear, a good case could be made for a date as early as the 9th century, when the kingdom of Scots is first securely established.

At the same time, the tensions between different parts of Scotland, most notably that between the highlands and the lowlands – itself a function of geography – is also part of the story. Just as Scotland is different, it harbours differences within. In addition, the long coastline has made the country notably susceptible to seaborne influences. The Gaelic west and the Viking north were evidence of this, although landward influences from the south – especially from the Normans onwards – proved most decisive of all.

Scottish history has inspired many legends and much mythology. Every nation needs such things. Legend and myth are anterior to history and without them there might be no history at all. They satisfy the imagination. But they can also take dramatic liberties with the known facts. Robert the Bruce, Mary Queen of Scots, John Knox and Bonnie Prince Charlie – just to name the better known examples – have all had this treatment from novelists, film makers and other popularisers. In doing my best to stick to the facts, I can only promise the reader that the history seems to me to make as good a story as any myth or legend.

Scotland c.1000 a.d.

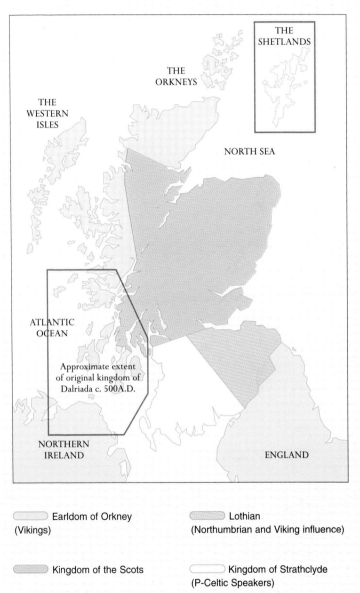

THE SHETLANDS

THE ORKNEYS

THE WESTERN ISLES

NORTH SEA

ATLANTIC OCEAN

Approximate extent of original kingdom of Dalriada c. 500A.D.

NORTHERN IRELAND

ENGLAND

Earldom of Orkney (Vikings)

Lothian (Northumbrian and Viking influence)

Kingdom of the Scots

Kingdom of Strathclyde (P-Celtic Speakers)

SCOTLAND

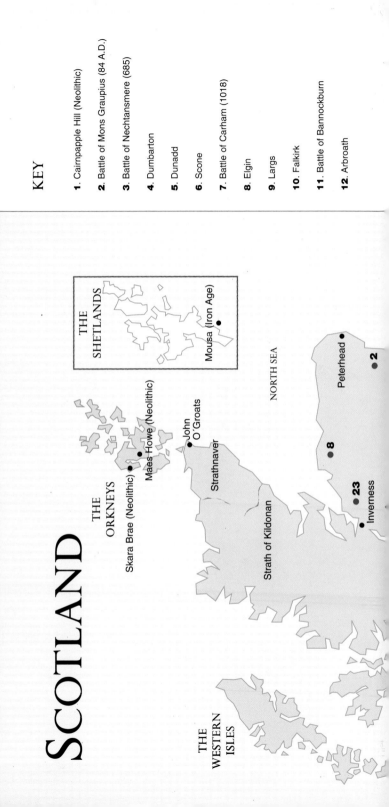

THE
WESTERN
ISLES

THE
ORKNEYS

Skara Brae (Neolithic)

Maes Howe (Neolithic)

John
O'Groats

Strathnaver

Strath of Kildonan

THE
SHETLANDS

Mousa (Iron Age)

NORTH SEA

Peterhead

2

8

23

Inverness

KEY

1. Cairnpapple Hill (Neolithic)

2. Battle of Mons Graupius (84 A.D.)

3. Battle of Nechtansmere (685)

4. Dumbarton

5. Dunadd

6. Scone

7. Battle of Carham (1018)

8. Elgin

9. Largs

10. Falkirk

11. Battle of Bannockburn

12. Arbroath

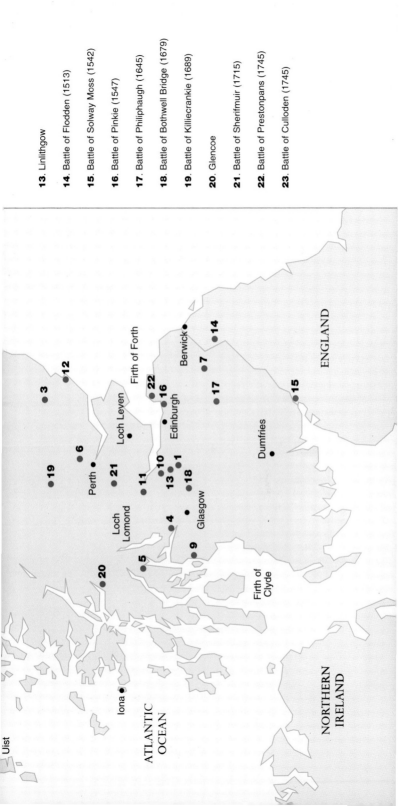

13. Linlithgow

14. Battle of Flodden (1513)

15. Battle of Solway Moss (1542)

16. Battle of Pinkie (1547)

17. Battle of Philiphaugh (1645)

18. Battle of Bothwell Bridge (1679)

19. Battle of Killiecrankie (1689)

20. Glencoe

21. Battle of Sherifmuir (1715)

22. Battle of Prestonpans (1745)

23. Battle of Culloden (1745)

1. PREHISTORIC SCOTLAND

In common with the rest of north-west Europe, Scotland was gradually populated by nomadic people from the south at the end of the great Ice Age, about 7000 B.C. These shadowy people were hunter-gatherers who probably settled for the most part in the more accessible coastal regions of the east, from the Firth of Forth to the Moray Firth, and in the Western Isles.

The location of these Mesolithic settlements is a pointer to two central features in Scottish history. First, the sea was a highway, not a barrier. The real impediment to movement lay inland where the highland massif made overland transport difficult, if not impossible. Second, the crucial geographical division between highland and lowland was there from the very start and is still there today. It has affected Scottish history culturally, linguistically and politically.

The first people who have left us physical evidence of their presence in Scotland are the Neolithic or New Stone Age settlers who began to arrive around 4500 B.C. As they gradually penetrated north from Europe into the British Isles, following the paths of their Mesolithic predecessors, they were able to establish permanent communities because they had agricultural skills.

Skara Brae

They knew how to cultivate grain, how to fish and how to keep animals.

This Neolithic incursion was not unique to Scotland. Indeed it is best to think of Scotland not as a separate entity but simply as a regional entity within the British Isles as a whole. The reasons why Scotland later acquired a more pronounced individual identity, culminating in its modern status as a distinct nation, will emerge in the course of this history. For the moment, it is enough to acknowledge that Neolithic Scotland has left us great archaeological survivals like the passage grave at Maes Howe on Orkney which dates from around 3000 B.C. Its similarities to passage graves in Ireland and Wales point to a common insular culture.

Maes Howe

Other archaeological survivals which bear witness to the settled nature of Stone Age society are Skara Brae on Orkney, one of the very finest examples of Neolithic domestic settlement in all of Europe, and Cairnpapple Hill in West Lothian. This site was occupied by a succession of people starting in Neolithic times – about 3000 B.C. – and continuing through the Bronze Age and into the Iron Age, which began in Scotland around 700 B.C.

Cairnpapple Hill

The Ring of Brogar stone circle, a pre-historic survival in Orkney

> *The Scots are beset by Scottish history: they cherish it, but have no use for it.*
>
> Iain Finlayson

The Bronze Age deepened the pattern, by now well established, whereby Scotland was part of a culture common to the network of islands off the European mainland. It had no separate identity, no more than England or Wales. Yet bronze ornaments from all over the British Isles were prized as luxuries in mainland Europe and we can be certain that some of these originated in Scotland.

The Bronze Age yielded to the Iron Age, brought to the British Isles by new waves of settlers from central Europe, the Celts. It is quite possible that the existing inhabitants of Scotland were themselves Celtic, but their origins are uncertain. The new wave of Iron Age Celts swept all before them, using the superior technology – especially in arms – which iron smelting afforded.

2. THE CELTS

With the arrival of the Iron Age Celts, we begin the journey from pre-history. It is not until the arrival of the Romans in Britain in the first century A.D. that we have surviving written documentation – as distinct from archaeological evidence – upon which we can rely. But at least Roman documents have left us a description of the societies they found throughout the entire island. Those societies were tribal, ruled by military aristocracies, spoke Celtic languages and built fortified positions to protect the non-military population. Their art employed motifs and techniques similar to Celtic societies on the continent.

There was a significant division in the greater world of the Celts which was to be important for the later history of Scotland. Two principal divisions had emerged in the original Celtic language, P-Celtic and Q-Celtic. Where the p sound occurred in one variant, there was a q or k sound in the other. The Celts who settled on the island of Britain were P-Celtic speakers; those who settled in Ireland spoke Q-Celtic. It is not certain to what extent the two languages were mutually comprehensible, although we know that they drifted apart more and more as the centuries wore on.

Before the Romans came to the island we now call Britain, a pattern was developing which is with us to this day. The low, flat fertile plains south of the Trent and east of the Severn were growing in wealth and population. These were the parts of Celtic Britain closest to its continental cousins and so best placed for trade. Towns such as St Albans and Colchester date from Celtic times.

It was also the region best placed for new migrants, new ideas and new technologies. The more upland and northerly regions, including Scotland – and especially those areas above the highland line – were slower to develop. For instance, population growth appears to have been sluggish. There seems to have been a series of internal migrations to the richer lands of southern Britain. Towns developed in the south,

△ Remains of the broch of Birsay, a Norse settlement on Orkney

▽ Rousay, a 1st-century broch on Orkney

An aerial view of Edin's Hall broch in the Borders

designed for trade rather than mere defence, and capable of establishing political control over very wide areas. In the northern upland areas, the hilltop fortification remained the norm. This was a local, tribal society based on stable and small-scale social relationships.

This contrast in Celtic Britain, between the lowland south and the upland north and west, was largely the result of geography. Good flat land and proximity to the continent were the determining factors. None the less, any modern Scot – or anyone from Yorkshire or Durham for that matter – will smile ruefully at the presence of a pattern, already

The broch on Mousa in the Shetland Islands

identifiable at the very dawn of history, which is one of the great recurring themes of Scottish and British life.

The surviving artifacts from this period of Iron Age settlement in northern Britain are not numerous. But they include the celebrated brochs, large dry-stone towers usually built on a coastal site, which have not been found outside Scotland. The finest example is on the uninhabited island of Mousa, in the Shetland group. The basic purpose of these structures appears to have been defensive.

But Celtic society throughout Britain was about to meet with a force against which it had no defence except distance. In 43 A.D., the Roman general Claudius – later emperor – landed a raiding party in southern Britain. By the late 70s the Romans had conquered all of modern England and Wales up to the line of the Cheviot hills. Then a new Roman governor was appointed, and he fixed his eye on the land further north. His name was Gnaeus Julius Agricola.

3. Roman Scotland

We are fortunate in knowing quite a lot about Agricola. His daughter was married to the great historian Tacitus, who has left a biography of him. He was born in Gaul, served in Britain as a young officer and was therefore well acquainted with the island when he returned to assume command.

In 80 and 81 he launched his legions across the Cheviots. A western column marched up Annandale, an eastern one up Lauderdale. Although the Celtic tribes knew of their approach, they did not unite against them. The Celtic preference for local autonomy denied them the opportunity to bring force of numbers and their intimate knowledge of the rough terrain to bear against the Romans. The result was that the two branches of Agricola's army effected a junction at Inveresk, on the Firth of Forth just east of where Edinburgh stands today.

From this position, Agricola quickly secured the country south of the Clyde-Forth line, including Galloway, where the local tribes were particularly bellicose. In 83 he pushed further north along the east coast and in the following year won a major battle against the Highland tribes at a position which Tacitus – who is the only surviving source we have for all this – calls Mons Graupius. This appears to have been Bennachie near the modern town of Inverurie in Aberdeenshire.

It was the high-water mark of Roman incursion.

▷ *A bust of the emperor Hadrian*

▽ *Hadrian's Wall at Cuddy's Cragg, near Housesteads in Northumberland*

The sunken remains of the Antonine Wall

Agricola was recalled to Rome shortly thereafter and no further effort was made to disturb the tribes in their highland fastnesses. The line of fortifications which Agricola had constructed to contain the tribes was allowed to decay. The Roman presence in southern Scotland was gradually pulled back farther and farther until the Emperor Hadrian, on his visit to Britain in 122, ordered the building of the great wall that was named for him along the Solway-Tyne line. This now marked the northern boundary of the empire.

For whatever reason – probably pressures from the northern tribes on Hadrian's Wall – Hadrian's imperial successor, Antoninus Pius, ordered a re-invasion. It proved to be the same old story. The Romans secured the line from the Clyde to the Firth of Forth, building a defensive wall known as the Antonine Wall which was maintained until the 160s and then abandoned.

Apart from one more brief incursion in the early third century, there was no further Roman attempt to conquer any part of Scotland. The Celtic tribes continued to harry the northern imperial boundaries through the long years of Roman decline. In 410, the Romans were withdrawn altogether from the island of Britain.

What was their legacy to Scotland? First, the idea of being separate. Hadrian's Wall was a boundary first and last, marking off the country beyond it as a place apart. Second, a restatement of the ancient highland-lowland division: Agricola conquered the latter, leaving the former unscathed. Third, the word Caledonia, used by Tacitus to describe the land north of the Forth. Finally, the word Picts, one of the most teasing words in Scottish history. It is a Roman word, from the

Dere Street, a Roman road in the Borders

Latin picti, painted people, and may refer to the practice of face-painting before a battle. At any rate, the Romans used it describe the tribes of Caledonia. We know remarkably little about them, or about their mysterious disappearance from history around the ninth century. As we shall see.

4. PICTS AND CELTS

Into the vacuum left by the Roman withdrawal from Britain, there moved not resurgent Celts but Germanic invaders. These Anglo-Saxons gradually occupied all of Roman Britain south of the Forth, except for Wales, Cornwall and Strathclyde (a region embracing large parts of south-west Scotland with its capital at Dumbarton and running down to modern Cumbria in England), where P-Celtic cultures survived. North of the Forth, the Picts still held sway.

A Pictish symbol stone, at the rock of broch of Birsay in Orkney

Meanwhile, raiders from the kingdom in Dalriada in north-east Ireland established a sister kingdom in Argyll (from the Gaelic Oirear Gael, shore of the Gaels) which they also named Dalriada: once again, the sea was a highway not a barrier. The Romans, who knew Ireland although they never invaded it, called these people the Scotti, hence the English words Scots and Scotland. The Dalriadans, like all the Irish Celts, spoke Q-Celtic or Gaelic, which was now introduced to the Scottish mainland. Not only did they bring their language: they also brought Christianity.

The story of Scotland between the departure of the Romans and the arrival of the Vikings in the late eighth century contains three inter-related themes: first, the failure of attempts by the newly arrived Anglo-Saxon tribes of the south to penetrate into Pictish territory; second, the gradual establishment, consolidation and expansion of the Gaelic-speaking people of Dalriada at the expense of the Picts; third, the spread of Christianity.

The Anglo-Saxons followed the classic east coast invasion route through Northumbria and into Lothian. By the late seventh century they had established their presence as far north as the Forth. They had clashed with the kingdoms of Strathclyde (P-Celts) and Dalriada (Q-Celts) in turn, but while they squeezed the boundaries of the former relentlessly towards the west and south, they made no attempt to invade the latter. Indeed, their relationship with the Dalriadans was complex, for Dalriada had become the centre of the Christian world in the northern part of Britain and many of the Anglo-Saxon tribes, especially those established in Northumbria, had been evangelised from Iona.

But whatever about the various Celtic groups in the west, the Anglo-Saxons had no compunction about

A Pictish scab and chape which dates from the 8th century

A naked Pict warrior, as imagined by a 16th-century English engraver

the Picts to their north. Just like Agricola almost six centuries earlier, they crossed the Forth and the Tay and came to battle at Nechtansmere, near the modern town of Forfar, in 685. That was as far as they got: the Picts inflicted a crushing defeat on them. The Anglo-Saxons never renewed their assault on Pictish territory. They settled for the presence they had established in Lothian and in those parts of eastern Strathclyde which they captured. Once again, the highland-lowland divide was at work: the highlands remained a fastness, the lowlands an outreach of the Northumbrian world to the south.

The pressure on the Picts eventually came not from the south but from the west. The Scotti of Dalriada, henceforth known to history as the Scots, gradually infiltrated their way into Pictish territory and established themselves all across the highlands. Gaelic displaced Pictish. At this point, the Picts disappear from our story. Of course, the people did not vanish but henceforth their descendants are referred to simply as Scots, as though they were Dalriadans. It has been said that Scottish history's two great unanswered questions are "Who exactly were the Picts?" and "What happened to them?" At any rate, the smaller entity had absorbed the greater: the snake had swallowed the pig.

The third development of the years 400-800, the coming of Christianity, requires a chapter to itself.

The hill fort at Dunadd in Argyll, an early stronghold in Dalriada

5. CHRISTIANITY

The first known Christian missionary to Scotland, St Ninian, established himself in Galloway early in the fifth century. His mission to the Picts may have penetrated as far as the Orkneys, but the evidence is sketchy. Moreover, he left little lasting impact.

His great successor, St Columba, was quite different, leaving an indelible mark upon the land that he won for the Christian faith. He was a Gael from Ireland, an aristocrat of Dalriadan stock, who founded a number of monasteries in his own country before crossing the sea

to Scotland with twelve companions in 563. Various reasons have been advanced for his leaving Ireland. The most common legend is that he fomented a quarrel which resulted in a great battle and that in his remorse for his conduct decided that he would sail out of sight of Ireland and redeem as many souls for Christ as had been killed at the battle.

He settled on the tiny island of Iona, off the Isle of Mull, out of sight of Ireland. From this improbable centre, he carried out a wholesale evangelisation of the Picts, helped by the friendship he formed with Brude mac Maelchon, the Pictish king whose seat was at Inverness. He was canny enough to preach a Christianity that was as compatible as possible with the existing Pictish religion, building churches at sacred sites and adapting Pictish festivals to the Christian church calendar.

His reach went beyond the Picts. Columba sent his monks across the lowlands and into Northumbria, introducing Christianity to the Anglo-Saxon tribes who had settled there. One of the great ironies of the Anglo-Saxon triumph in England is that these Germanic conquerors were pagans, whereas the Celtic peoples they displaced and drove west were already Christian because of the Roman presence. Now, however, Christianity was reintroduced to north-east England by Irish monks working from a Scottish base. Indeed, the Columban influence was felt much further south: of the first four bishops of Mercia (roughly the modern English counties of Cheshire, Staffordshire and Shropshire) three were either Irish or had been trained in Ireland.

△ *This detail from a 19th-century frieze of Scottish history shows St Ninian, the first Christian missionary*

▽ *A stained glass representation of St Columba*

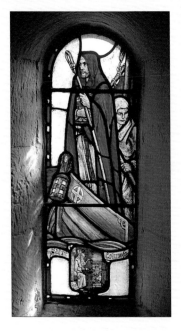

Columba died on Iona in 597 after a mission that had lasted thirty-four years. In that very year, at the other end of the island of Britain, the Italian St Augustine arrived from Rome with a party of forty monks charged by Pope Gregory I with the task of converting the Anglo-Saxons to Christianity and bringing them into full communion with Rome. He became the first Archbishop of Canterbury.

In Scotland, meanwhile, the work of conversion was already done. But the remote Columban church was out of line with Roman orthodoxy on a number of important issues, most notably the means employed to calculate the date of Easter. This led to much friction, especially as the Augustinian evangelisation of England pressed ever northward. Eventually, the Synod of Whitby in 664 drew concessions from the Columbans. But the vigour and integrity of the Columban church in Scotland was to remain for the best part of the next 500 years.

△ *An early Christian standing stone*

▽ *St Augustine, the first Archbishop of Canterbury*

6. KENNETH MACALPIN

The period from the death of Columba to the kingship of Kenneth I encompasses about 250 years. In that time, the Columban legacy established a common religious culture among the indigenous peoples north of the Tweed. The Scots of Dalriada; the Picts above the Forth-Clyde line; the P-Celtic speakers of Strathclyde; and the Anglo-Saxons in the Borders: all were Christian. It was the arrival of a new, intrusive and un-Christian force that caused the next upheaval.

△ *No image of Kenneth McAlpine survives. This is what a 19th-century engraver imagined he looked like*

Lindisfarne, Holy Island, off the coast of Northumberland

The Vikings first announced themselves in 793, when they destroyed the famous monastery at Lindisfarne, off the Northumbrian coast. The following year they sacked Iona, wrecking its famous library. In the early years of the ninth century, they maintained relentless pressure on Dalriada, edging the Scots eastwards.

At the same time, the Picts felt the weight of Viking arms. Orkney and Shetland were early casualties and the invaders managed to establish colonies in the far north and in the Hebrides.

There were, therefore, good reasons for the Scots and the Picts to move closer together. They were both Christian people threatened by a common pagan enemy. The apparent union was really a takeover by the Scots. The Picts suffered a massive defeat at the hands of the Vikings in 839 which in turn left them vulnerable to the ambitions of the Scots. And those ambitions were personified in the figure of Kenneth MacAlpin (Cionnaith mac Ailpin), who ascended the throne of Dalriada in the same year.

By whatever means – we simply don't know – he also became king of the Picts four years later. He immediately abandoned the old Dalriadan capital of Dunadd, just north of the modern town of Lochgilphead in Argyll, and established himself in the ancient Pictish centre of Scone in Perthshire. From Iona he brought the remains of St Columba, which he re-interred at the monastery of Dunkeld. He also brought the celebrated Stone of Destiny, a red sandstone block variously reputed to have been the biblical Jacob's pillow and St Columba's writing desk. For the next four and a half centuries it was the sacred coronation stone of the Scots until King Edward I of England stole it. Kenneth established Scone and Dunkeld – they are about twenty miles apart – as the civil and ecclesiastical capitals of his new unified kingdom. The triumph of the

Scots probably disguises the extent of early Pictish resistance to the new arrangements. Although we have no reliable estimates of population, we can be certain that the Picts were much more numerous, which makes their eventual absorption all the more mysterious. Yet absorbed they were. As we have already noted, Gaelic ousted Pictish. It was probably helped to do so by Gaelic's position as the language of Scotland's Christian heartland, Dalriada, and therefore as the prestige language of literacy and scholarship. None the less, its swift displacement of Pictish is remarkable. It now became the establishment language of the court, of the law, of commerce.

Kenneth MacAlpin was the first king of Scotland and the common ancestor of every Scottish king for the next 500 years. But he was not king of all modern Scotland. He never established himself in the Borders, where the Anglo-Saxon Northumbrians continued to hold sway, nor did he absorb the old kingdom of Strathclyde, although the Scots captured Dumbarton in 870. The real anxiety for the new kingdom of Scotland came not from the south but the north. For it was from there that the Vikings came, in wave after wave. Few people have had a more profound effect on Scottish history.

△ Whithorn Priory, in Dumfries, the centre of St Ninian's Christian mission to Scotland in the 5th century. This building dates from the 12th century

▽ Iona Abbey

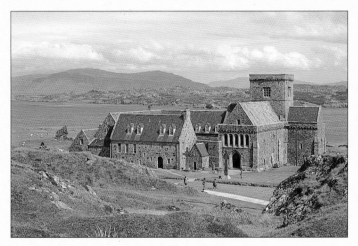

7. The Vikings

Viking power was a product of technology. They were astonishing seafarers with a genius for ship design. Their narrow, shallow-draughted longships were the fastest, most manoeuvrable craft of their day, capable not only of covering great distances but also of transporting fighting men to distant places. They swept across north-west Europe: if ever a people used the sea as a highway it was the Vikings. They conquered much of eastern England; they founded all of modern Ireland's cities and coastal towns; they colonised Normandy and much of the southern Baltic littoral; they founded the oldest of all trading centres in the Russian interior, Novgorod. They probably discovered North America. And in Scotland they settled the far north and the islands.

△ *The Gokstad ship, a good example of a Viking longship*

▽ *The remains of the Jarlshof Viking settlement on Shetland*

The Vikings completely overwhelmed Pictish culture in Orkney and Shetland and on the mainland in Sutherland and Caithness. The name "Sutherland" is itself of Scandinavian origin. It simply means "south land", which is exactly what it was to the people who so named it. The fact that it is practically the most northerly part of the island of Britain is neither here nor there. Northern Scotland is littered with place-names of Scandinavian origin, as are the Hebrides and the Western

A Viking disc brooch

Somerled, who displaced the Gaelic Dalriadans from part of Argyll. The name Somerled, in turn, became gaelicised as Somhairle and anglicised as Sorley. The Viking inheritance may be occluded but it is there.

The Vikings who settled in Scotland were mainly Norwegian in origin. They were a new addition to the ethnic mix in northern Britain, complementing the Scots and Picts, the Northumbrians and the P-Celts of Strathclyde. By 1000 A.D., what we know as Scotland still only existed in embryo. Nor was there anything

Isles whose relationship one to the other was ideal for seaborne settlers like the Vikings.

The sea was crucial. Apart from eastern England with its great navigable rivers like the Humber, the Trent and the Thames, they seldom settled far inland. In Scotland, they did not venture beyond the highlands and islands. They did not attempt to conquer the kingdom of the Scots to the south, but they did establish successful colonies in the north. Gradually, they adapted to Gaelic ways, speaking the language, inter-marrying and adopting the kinship system based on clans chacteristic of the Scots. (Indeed, its remote origins go back to Pictish times.) Some of Scotland's most famous clan names, among them MacDonald and MacDougal, are of Viking not Gaelic origin. The original Donald and Dougal were grandsons of one

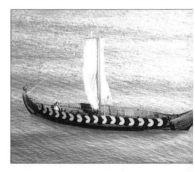

A reconstructed Viking longship at sea

determining that it should come into existence in the form that it did. History could just as easily have worked out differently, with Viking colonies in the highlands and islands linked to a wider Scandinavian seaborne empire; a Scottish kingdom in the old heartland of the southern Picts north of the Forth-Clyde line and south of Caithness and Sutherland; and an English sphere of influence reaching to the Firth of Forth. Indeed this would have been consistent with much of Scottish history up until then, especially in the lowlands. But of course it did not work out like that.

The placename 'Dingwall' near the Moray Firth is the same as 'Thingwall' on the coast of Lancashire, both names illustrating the influence of the Vikings in northern Britain.

Hugh Kearney

---

8. Malcolm and Margaret

The kingship established by Kenneth MacAlpin in 843 was Gaelic. One of the most peculiar customs of the Gaels, alike in Scotland and Ireland, was their arrangement for the royal succession. A king might be succeeded by any of his male relatives who shared a common great-grandfather. Compared to the old Picts or the Anglo-Saxons to the south, where succession was through the first-born in the female and male line respectively, the Scots' arrangements seem crazy. Yet they

Dunfermline Abbey and Palace, a Benedictine abbey founded by Queen Margaret

had a certain logic. They were an extension of the kinship system which was focused on the tribe or clan and they allowed for a meritocracy among qualified candidates.

Fatally, the system also allowed for contested kingships. Thus it was that seven successive kings, from Malcolm I to Kenneth III, died violently. Their combined reigns covered only sixty-two years.

The Scots finally got a king who reigned for a generation, Malcolm II (1005-34). He won the battle of Carham (1018) against the Anglo-Saxons of Lothian, thus capturing this long-disputed region and extending his kingdom to the Tweed. He effectively extinguished the autonomy of Strathclyde and at the end of his life it passed into the inheritance of his grandson and successor, Duncan I. The lowlands were Scottish for the first time.

Duncan was headstrong. He led an ill-starred invasion of Northumbria which ended in disaster and then fomented what was a kind of civil war by threatening the regional liberties of his kingdom. The Scots, like all peoples whose basis was the kinship group, valued local freedoms and resented any threat of overweening central authority. Duncan was slain in battle by Macbeth who then succeeded him and ruled wisely from 1040 to 1057. (Shakespeare's portrayal of Macbeth is an historical travesty from beginning to end.) Yet he too died violently at the hands of one of Duncan's sons who succeeded as Malcolm III, known to history as Malcolm Canmore (from the Gaelic ceann mor, big head).

Malcolm Canmore had grown up in England and Normandy, having fled Scotland following his father's deposition. His English connections were useful to him in gaining the Scottish throne although he repaid the English not at all, repeatedly invading south of the Tweed. He was a wild, hard-drinking, uncouth warrior. He also married a revolutionary, for in 1070, he married Margaret, a princess of the Anglo-Saxon royal house which had been ousted by the Norman conquest four years earlier. She introduced southern refinements to the Scottish court. More importantly, she introduced the Anglo-Saxon language which in time developed into lowlands Scots. It became the official language of the kingdom and the common speech of the lowlands until the eighteenth century. To the great resentment of highlanders, Gaelic had begun its long decline.

The queen was also an enthusiastic religious reformer, deploring the particularities of the remote Scottish church, still basically Columban in form. She began the decline of the Columban church as she began the decline of Gaelic. Henceforth, the Christian church in Scotland would follow Roman ways for over four centuries.

Malcolm Canmore died in battle in 1093 and his remarkable queen seemed to lose the will to live when she heard the news. She had introduced England and Europe into the Scottish equation with greater urgency than ever before through her political, linguistic and ecclesiastical innovations. England itself was by now an extension of Europe, for it had been conquered and settled by the Normans. And they were heading relentlessly north.

△ *Kildalton Cross on the island of Islay is the finest Scottish high cross which survives from the 9th and 10th centuries*

▽ *Chapel Finian, five miles north-west of Fort William in Dunfries, a pilgrimage church which dates from about 1000 AD*

9. The Norman Lowlands

The Normans were the descendants of Viking settlers who had colonised the province of Normandy in the ninth century. In England, their invasion of 1066 is usually called the Norman Conquest. Colonisation might be a better word, for essentially it was a colonising enterprise which established a new French-speaking elite to dominate the indigenous peoples. This model is particularly appropriate in the case of Norman Scotland.

Malcolm III's descendants were the principal instruments in the Norman settlement of the lowlands. The new Scottish kingship was lowland based and strongly influenced by English customs and manners. To that extent, it was resented in the highlands. These lowland kings in turn wished their writs to run as far as possible in the highlands and for this they needed military help from England.

The Norman settlement of the lowlands was, therefore, fundamentally different from that in England. It happened not by invasion but by royal invitation. It was sponsored by the Scottish monarchy to secure military aid and modernise an archaic kingdom.

The Normans brought four main institutions to Scotland, of which feudalism was the most important. Feudalism was a system in which land was granted in return for rent or military service. This presupposed that the person making the grant actually owned the land in the first place. Thus feudalism was implicitly hierarchical and at the head of the hierarchy was the king. But such a system, while efficient and extremely profitable for the magnates in whose interests it operated, was as remote as one

Bothwell Castle, a Norman castle dating from the 13th century

Castle Sween, on the eastern shore of Loch Sween near Tarbert in Argyll, is one of the earliest Norman stone castles in Scotland, dating from the mid 12th-century

could imagine from the kinship-based models of common ownership which still obtained in the highlands.

The other three Norman institutions were all agents of social control. First there was the fortified castle, which defended the new colonial arrangements and protected the magnates with a permanent show of overwhelming force. Second, there were the chartered towns or boroughs which provided local centres of trade and commerce. Finally there was the modernised church, fully in communion with Roman orthodoxy.

All this turned the lowlands into a society organised along contemporary continental lines, with a centralised government and legal system, a uniform coinage and a Romanised church. The highlands, on the other hand, retained their old Gaelic particularities. Government was diffused through the kinship group of the clan; justice was not reckoned on the basis of individual guilt but of collective responsibility, with the terrors of the vendetta as the ultimate guarantor of good behaviour; Columban church practices such as married clergy survived long after they had been reformed out of existence in the lowlands.

The highland-lowland rift was deepened by the Canmore line of kings and by the Norman settlement. In particular, the durability of the clan system was an affront to generations of Scottish monarchs, for its fundamental principles were inimical to centralised royal government. But for the moment and for centuries to come, the clan chiefs ruled the highlands.

A detail from Bayeux Tapestry showing the death of King Harold at the Battle of Hastings, the decisive battle in the Norman conquest of England

It is over simplistic, all the same, to see the Normans simply as invaders and colonisers. The country that we know as Scotland is ultimately more their creation than that of the highlanders. Some of Scotland's most famous family names are Norman: Fraser, Lindsay, Grant, Sinclair, Hamilton, Leslie and Lennox; likewise the two royal houses of Bruce and Stewart. In the twelfth century, the Scotland we think of now did not exist. But the Normans began the process of nation-making by imposing themselves on the lowlands and then, as far as possible, imposing lowland ways on the highlands.

10. CONSOLIDATION AND CRISIS

Norman Scotland was just a small part of a wider Norman imperial world that embraced the British Isles, Normandy itself and the huge French province of Aquitaine. As with other parts of the Norman world, a French-speaking ruling class was overlaid on a native population which spoke an indigenous tongue. In the lowlands, this was Scots; in the highlands, Gaelic.

These relationships were not static. Just as the Vikings in the highlands adapted themselves to Gaelic ways, the Gaels themselves felt the impact of feudalism which at least modified without wholly usurping the traditional ties of kinship on which Gaelic society rested. This process was neither linear nor painless: there were numerous local rebellions in the highlands protesting against the erosion of traditional liberties and practices and in some cases challenging the legitimacy of the Canmore dynasty itself.

By the end of the twelfth century, the Norman hold on the lowlands and the east of Scotland – the traditional invasion route from ancient times – was secure. As in all the other Norman lands, great abbeys and cathedrals were built to mark the spiritual progress of the conquest. Their foundation dates are all within the first 150 years of the Norman incursion: Holyrood (1128), St Andrews (1160, completed 1318), Elgin (1224), St Giles, Edinburgh (1243). In addition, David I and his successors introduced new continental religious orders such as the Augustinians and the Cistercians and established the ten Scottish bishoprics. As elsewhere in Europe, episcopacy was an instrument of royal power.

In the thirteenth century, the Scottish kings attempted to extend their rule west and north from this central heartland. Galloway remained stubbornly autonomous,

◁ *The remains of St Andrew's cathedral in Fife*

▽ *Holyrood Palace in Edinburgh was originally founded in the 12th century. The present building dates from the 17th century*

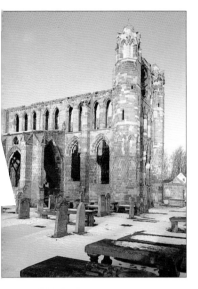

Elgin cathedral

reflecting its mixed P-Celtic, Irish and Viking inheritance and its happy remoteness from Edinburgh. But they had better fortune against the Vikings in Argyll and the islands. By a mixture of cajoling, bribery and threats, Alexander II (1214-49) and Alexander III (1249-86) tried to loosen the Viking grip. Finally, the earl of Ross invaded Skye – almost certainly with royal approval – and this strike into the Viking heartland drew a fearsome response from King Haakon of Norway, the ultimate overlord of the Viking empire.

Haakon assembled a huge invasion force but met with disaster when a storm scattered his fleet at the Battle of Largs in the Firth of Clyde in 1263. He died on the retreat to Norway and Alexander III concluded a peace treaty with his successor Magnus which brought the western islands within the Scots' royal domain.

Alexander died suddenly without a male heir in 1286. He was the last of the house of Canmore and the last king of Scotland to claim lineal descent from Kenneth MacAlpin. His only child, a daughter, had been married to the king of Norway but had died three years before giving birth to the infant who now succeeded Alexander, a four-year-old child called Margaret known to history as the Maid of Norway. She was already engaged to the son of King Edward I of England, a boy two years younger than herself, so that when they grew up and married there would have been a union of crowns. All this fell through in 1290 when Margaret died suddenly.

The crisis that followed operated on two levels. First, there was a factional struggle for the crown which eventually came down to a contest between two men, John Balliol and Robert Bruce of Annandale, both prominent members of the Norman aristocracy. Second, however, was the intervention of Edward I of England, a man of imperial vision and titanic energy.

A modern view of the town of Largs. The famous battle of 1283 in which Alexander III defeated the King of Norway was fought in these waters

11. HAMMER OF THE SCOTS

Scottish kings had paid feudal homage to English kings before the 1290s. As far back as 1174, William the Lion had acknowledged himself the formal vassal of Henry II. Such acts did not imply that Scotland was a dependency of England. In the first place, England and Scotland hardly existed in the modern sense. The age of centralised states with uniform laws, secure boundaries and centralised administration – all the things that we take completely for granted – lay well in the future. So when the king of Scots acknowledged the king of England as his feudal overlord, he may have done so in reparation for Scottish raids southwards or in his capacity as an English landholder – for the kings of Scots were also earls of Huntingdon since David I won the title as part of his marriage settlement in the 1120s.

None the less, English kings inevitably regarded themselves as

The Coronation Chair and the Stone of Scone

A medieval manuscript showing King Edward I of England with monks and bishops

superior to their Scottish counterparts. They were richer and their territories were larger. What was revolutionary about Edward I was that he tried to give permanent expression to all this.

As the middle ages advanced, kings tried to develop their feudal overlordship into something more concrete. It was the beginning of modern state building. They sought to extend their personal powers over wider and wider regions. Edward I was no exception. He was a tireless law maker and law enforcer. He pushed the effective boundaries of English royal power ever farther from the centre, conquering Wales in the 1280s. Edward's campaigns against the Scots can only be understood against this background. He was the first person to dream of a single, effective centre of royal power for all of the island of Britain.

When the throne of Scotland became vacant on the death of the Maid of Norway, the lowland nobles

accepted Edward as arbitrator between the claims of Balliol and Bruce. As the greatest feudal lord on the island, it seemed to feudal minds that he should settle the matter. But he himself had a mind that was outrunning the obligations of feudalism. The lowlands nobles thought that he would make his choice and then withdraw to the same distance that the kings of England had always kept. Edward had different ideas. Having made a royal progress through the lowlands, he chose Balliol as king in 1292 while claiming formal overlordship for himself and his successors.

Moreover, he had support in Scotland. Outside the lowlands, the king of Scots' writ did not always run. Even within the lowlands, not everybody was happy with the choice of Balliol. A major Scottish magnate, MacDuff of Fife, took a law case to the English courts against Balliol, who found himself answering at Westminster, under English law, in a case brought against him by one of his ostensible subjects.

Then came Edward's wars in France, as King Philip IV attempted to annex Aquitaine. Balliol, maddened by Edward's importunities, allied himself with the French. Edward responded by invading Scotland in 1296, defeating Balliol at Dunbar and overthrowing him. He then progressed right through Scotland – highlands and all – and returned home, taking the Stone of Scone with him, just to show who was boss. To underline the point, he held a parliament at Berwick where he received the homage of the Scots nobility.

There was no longer a king of Scots. Edward appeared to have realised his dream of insular unity. If he had succeeded, what we call Scotland would never have existed. It would have been a kind of Yorkshire beyond the Tweed. But Edward failed. The triumphs of 1296 represented the apogee of his power in the north. In the early fourteenth century the story took another twist.

△ Scots infantry man from the age of Edward I

▽ The harbour and ruined castle at Dunbar. It was near here that Edward I defeated Balliol in 1296

12. INDEPENDENCE

Edward I had two problems with Scotland. The first was distance, the same basic difficulty that had faced the Romans more than a thousand years earlier. It was too big and too remote for effective rule from London: how were taxes to be levied and collected or the king's laws enforced? It was the same problem that the kings of Scots had themselves encountered. As far as Edward was concerned, some local magnates in the lowlands might be relied upon but not all. The

Scots, wha hae wi Wallace bled,
Scots, wham Bruce has aften
led, –
Welcome to your gory bed, –
Or to victorie.

Robert Burns
'Robert Bruce's March to Bannockburn'

highlands were fiercely independent. This was Edward's second problem. Just at what point Scottish particularism of every sort begins to change into a kind of early nationalism, defined by and developing in opposition to the growing power of the neighbouring English state, is not certain. The kingdom of Scots had been a fact of life for almost 500 years. Although it had never held all of what is now Scotland, it had consistently been the biggest political unit; its heartland and traditions were secure; its royal succession had been orderly for the most part. With the coming of Norman feudalism, it had acknowledged the nominal overlordship of the English kings as part of a theoretical feudal hierarchy. But none of this impinged on day-to-day affairs until Edward I attempted to turn theory into practice. The subsequent campaigns of Wallace and Bruce were designed to defend traditional arrangements. Edward, meanwhile, tried to bully the Scots into a united kingdom focused on London – as he had already successfully done with the Welsh – and in failing he inevitably heightened the Scots' sense of their own distinctiveness.

But Scotland was not a nation – yet. That lay in the future, although the resistance to Edward I contained the seeds of nationalism. In essence, it was an inter-Norman quarrel. For instance, the Robert Bruce of Annandale who had been Balliol's rival for the throne was a Norman – the family was originally from Brix in

The Bruce Monument, Bannockburn

Normandy – and it was his grandson who was to gain the victory of Bannockburn which confirmed him as king of Scots.

The first revolt against Edward came under the leadership of William Wallace, the son of a Renfrewshire gentleman. He won a notable victory over the English at Stirling Bridge in September 1297 but within a year Edward had avenged this defeat at the Battle of Falkirk. Wallace fled to France. When he returned in 1305 he was betrayed and executed. Many of the Scots-Norman magnates accepted Edward's rule

A 19th-century representation of the Battle of Bannockburn

and had paid homage to him at a parliament held at St Andrews in 1304.

With Wallace dead, the leadership of Scots opposition passed into the hands of Robert Bruce (1274-1329), grandson of the contender of 1292. In 1306 he claimed the throne of Scots, vacant since the rout of Balliol ten years earlier. After a long campaign in which he faced many internal enemies as well as the English, he finally triumphed. He was

This fine sandstone statue of William Wallace stands in the Eildon hills in the Borders

helped by the death of Edward I in 1307 and his succession by his feckless and epicene son.

Bruce managed to build a coalition of Scots whose common denominator was fear of domination by a distant power. By 1309 he was strong enough to hold a parliament at St Andrews and to claim the recognition of the king of France. His military campaigns gradually put such pressure on the English that Edward II was finally obliged to send a formidable army north to relieve Stirling Castle, beseiged by the king's brother Edward Bruce.

On midsummer day 1314, King Robert I and King Edward II met in battle at Bannockburn, near Stirling, and the Scot won a victory so decisive that it ended the English threat for the moment. More important, it became a mythic event in Scottish life: the battle which confirmed Scotland as an independent kingdom.

13. Reversals of Fortune

Robert reigned for fifteen years after Bannockburn. In 1318, he captured Berwick and secured the Borders. He gained international recognition for his throne. The Declaration of Arbroath (1320) was a powerful assertion of Scottish independence, made in a letter addressed to the pope in the names of thirty-nine Scots noblemen in an attempt to counter pro-English propaganda in Rome. It worked: the pope recognised the independence of Bruce's kingdom, an important victory in pre-Reformation Europe, for the pope was the supreme head of the Christian world. In a sense, he was the ultimate feudal overlord. In 1328, the year before his death, Bruce signed the Treaty of Northampton with the young King Edward III, in which the English king formally recognised the claim of the

The seal of King Robert of Scotland

king of Scots. Yet within a few years of King Robert's death, most of these gains had been frittered away.

Edward III of England hated the Treaty of Northampton, which he regarded as a document signed under duress. Then King Robert died. He was succeeded by his son David II, a five year old. Edward III saw his chance. He encouraged the ambitions of Edward Balliol, son of the former king. Balliol invaded Scotland but was repulsed after some initial success, whereupon Edward III promptly repudiated the Treaty of Northampton. He led a royal army north, with the wretched Balliol tagging along in his wake, and routed the Scots at Halidon Hill near Berwick in 1333. David fled to France. Edward installed Balliol as puppet king and re-established English power throughout Lothian and the lowlands in a manner that would have been more than pleasing to his ferocious grandfather.

Then in 1337 the English involvement in France changed

King Edward III of England

King Robert and his first wife

everything, as it had done in the 1290s. The growing French kingdom wanted to incorporate Aquitaine, a Plantagenet possession since 1152. A series of wars, known collectively as the Hundred Years War, now began. Most early success went to the English, especially at the great battle of Crecy (1346). The French, under extreme pressure after Crecy, asked King David – who had returned to Scotland in 1341 – to mount a diversionary attack on the north of England. He did so, but was defeated in Northumbria, captured and led off to the Tower of London as a prisoner.

He was not released for over ten years. In the meantime, the Black Death had decimated the Scots population as it had done elsewhere in Europe. David died in 1371, to be succeeded by his nephew Robert, hereditary high steward of Scotland, who took the family name Stewart.

Edward III, absorbed by his continental adventure, effectively turned his back on Scotland, preferring to seek victory in France. Precarious though it was, the independence of the Scottish kingdom was now a fact. There was to be much border skirmishing and much enmity in the years to come but never again a wholesale attempt to absorb Scotland into a greater English state. Robert the Bruce's legacy was safe.

14. THE EARLY STEWARTS

S afe but shaky. The history of Scotland from the accession of Robert II in 1371 until the Reformation is a guignol of intrigue, faction and murder mixed with solid achievement. Essential to any understanding of this period is the knowledge that Scots independence was underwritten by the French. This was the famous Auld Alliance, which went back to John Balliol in the 1290s. However, it had the effect of turning the borders into a perennial theatre of war.

The early Stewarts continued the attempts of their Canmore predecessors to widen the reach of royal power and to reduce that of regional magnates. In this, they were in line with developments in English and continental kingships but it inevitably led to crises. Powerful lowland families like the Douglases controlled vast areas of land. With land went wealth, men, arms and power. The Scottish kings had to balance their desire to rule effectively with a recognition that that rule was often best accomplished through the agency of families like the Douglases. Moreover, the Douglas heartland was in Galloway, a region which had for centuries been semi-detached from the Scottish crown.

▷ *King James I*

▽ *Doune Castle the stronghold of the Duke of Albany, Regent of Scotland in the early 15th century*

King James III

The major figure in the early fifteenth century was the duke of Albany, younger brother of Robert III, who was appointed lieutenant of the kingdom in 1402. When his brother died in 1406, he continued in his position, becoming regent during the minority of the new king, James I, who was only ten on his father's death. Moreover, the boy king was a prisoner of the English who had captured him at sea while he was en route to France, presumably for schooling.

Albany was effectively king of Scotland for almost twenty years. He died in 1420, to be succeeded briefly by his son Murdoch. Then, in 1424, James I came home from England and was crowned at Scone. He turned violently against the great magnates. Murdoch, Duke of Albany, was executed. The 5th earl of Douglas was imprisoned. Highland chiefs, among them Alexander MacDonald, the Lord of the Isles, were invited to a dinner in Inverness and were promptly arrested. Some, although not Alexander, were murdered. The crown of Scotland was still not strong enough to take on the lordship of the isles, although it did so later in the century.

James I was finally murdered by disgruntled subjects in 1437, to be succeeded by his son James II, who was still a minor. That curse of medieval Scottish kingships, a regency, was once again required. This time it lasted twelve years in the hands of a succession of Douglases, who naturally used their time to advance their own interests at the expense of other powerful families. But once James reached his majority he showed himself a king in his father's mould.

He finally broke the power of the Douglases in the 1450s, using a key new development – artillery – to attack their castles which were now no longer invulnerable. His successor, James III, employed similar weaponry against the MacDonalds of the isles, finally reducing the lordship in 1476. James IV formally assumed the title Lord of the Isles in the 1490s, making a royal progress through the islands to underline the point. Orkney and Shetland drifted into the ambit of the kings of Scots, having been pledged as a royal dowry when James III married Margaret, daughter of King Christian I of Norway and Denmark in 1468. Gradually but inexorably, the kingdom of Scots was pushing ever outward. What we call Scotland was being born.

The countryside in Galloway, a region which traditionally protected its independence from central authority

15. END OF THE MIDDLE AGES

Scottish independence had been consolidated because England was busy in France fighting the Hundred Years War. Subsequently, it had been embroiled in the long civil war known as the Wars of the Roses. This gave the medieval kings of Scots the breathing space they needed. They put it to good use in reducing the power of their own regional magnates, just as the kings of England and France were doing in their countries. Thus Scotland became a dominant kingdom in its own right, not a subservient region.

Mary of Guise, the Queen Regent and mother of Mary Queen of Scots

James II died when one of his beloved artillery pieces exploded during the siege of Roxburgh Castle in 1460. James III survived plots against him by his brothers and various Douglases before eventually being murdered in 1488. James III is remembered more as a patron of the arts than a warrior king: he is the first Scottish king to whom the term Renaissance man might be applied. He built the great hall at Stirling and began work on the royal palace at Linlithgow. James IV reigned for a

quarter of a century until he perished along with the flower of Scotland's chivalry at the Battle of Flodden.

The Wars of the Roses ended in 1485 when Henry VII became the first Tudor king of England. Although never renewing the full English claim against Scotland, he encouraged attacks by English privateers in Scottish waters and gave support to the MacDonalds of the isles. In turn, the Scots supported pretenders to the English crown. Eventually, in 1503, a treaty of perpetual peace was signed by James IV and Henry VII. It was part of a marriage settlement, for the king of England gave his daughter Margaret's hand to the king of Scots.

The peace held. But when Henry VII died in 1509 and was replaced by the bombastic and ambitious Henry VIII, all was changed. Henry went to war with France, which promptly looked for Scottish support under the obligations of the Auld Alliance. Moreover, Henry had encouraged acts of English aggression in the borders in the hope of drawing the Scots into battle. James IV was in a quandary, caught between the treaty

Linlithgow Palace

with his wife's brother and the traditional alliance with the French. Despite the advice of most of his courtiers who favoured neutrality, he chose war with the English. The result was the disaster at Flodden (1513), the greatest defeat in Scottish history. Almost every noble household in the lowlands suffered a loss; significantly, many highlanders died as well. It was a national catastrophe, symbolised in the death of the king himself.

Flodden was just one – if the best remembered – of a succession of battles in the borders between the crowns of England and Scotland, the latter acting as a regional provocateur for its patron, France. But it was not simply part of a melancholy pattern. It sowed seeds of discontent with France and with the Auld Alliance which bore fruit two generations later.

The inner buildings at Stirling castle, an ancient centre of Scottish royal power

opened unknown reaches of the globe to European commerce and settlement. The year before Flodden, Michelangelo had finished painting the ceiling of the Sistine Chapel in Rome. In 1513 itself, Machiavelli began writing *The Prince*. And four years later, an obscure German monk called Martin Luther nailed his 95 theses to the door of Wittenberg Cathedral. The Protestant Reformation was the result, a revolutionary upheaval that left no part of Europe untouched. In Scotland, its effect was seismic.

The battle of Flodden

Although no one knew it then, Flodden marked the end of medieval Scotland. All of Europe was caught in the heady swirl of the high Renaissance. Printing by moveable type was the technological sensation of the age; the great voyages of discovery by Columbus, Vasco da Gama and Bartolomeu Diaz had

*Still from the sire the
son shall hear
Of the stern strife and
carnage drear,
Of Flodden's fatal field,
Where shiver'd was fair
Scotland's spear
And broken was her shield.*

**Sir Walter Scott
from *Marmion***

16. THE EARLY REFORMATION

With the death of his father at Flodden, the throne passed to James V. In the melancholy way of the Stewarts he was a minor. Following two confused regencies in which pro-French and pro-English interests clashed, James finally asumed full power in 1528.

James V was a popular king, but he hated faction and he further curtailed the ambitions of provincial magnates. He became the first king of Scots to sail right around his kingdom from the Firth of Forth anti-clockwise to the Clyde, visiting many islands and accepting the homage of local chieftains. In some cases, he even took hostages against the clans' good behaviour.

In the meantime, many of the lowland nobility whom the king had alienated were being attracted to the new doctrines of the Reformation. They were encouraged in this by Henry VIII of England, who had broken with Rome – although without

Henry VIII of England

himself embracing Protestantism: that came later – and was anxious to foment difficulties for the pro-French king of Scots. James V was a vigorous Catholic, staunchly defending the old faith. He did not scruple to burn Patrick Hamilton, an early reformer, at the stake in 1528. Moreover, his queen – Mary of Guise – was French, so that the coupling of Catholicism and the French alliance was ever strenghtened. In an equal and opposite way, early Scots reformers looked to England.

The Catholic Church in Scotland was rotten with corruption, absenteeism and an impoverished and ignorant clergy. It cried out for reform. But all reform came with political implications, which made it impossible while the pro-French party was in the ascendant. Henry VIII, meanwhile, felt under threat from Catholic states on the continent because of his break with the Pope. In turn, he feared a pro-French Scotland at his rear. He tried sweet reason, inviting James V to a meeting at York. James stood him up. In a fury, Henry launched his armies into the lowlands. An

King James V of Scotland

attempted counter-attack by the Scots ended in their craven surrender at Solway Moss in November 1542. This was followed shortly after by the death of James.

His six-day-old daughter Mary, the famous Queen of Scots, succeeded. Her mother, Mary of Guise, was regent. Henry VIII now tried to arrange a wedding between his young son Edward and the infant queen. A marriage alliance between England and Scotland would have trumped the Auld Alliance and relieved Henry's anxieties. To this end, he invaded Scotland again in the campaign known ever after as the "Rough Wooing". Despite yet another English victory at the battle of Pinkie (1547) it was all to no avail. The French party remained in control.

But the earth was moving beneath them, for the doctrines of the Reformation were making real headway in Scotland. Influenced by continental developments, disgusted at the abuses in the Roman church in Scotland and in some cases openly opposed to the French alliance, many lowland Scots in particular embraced reform. In 1546, the Protestant preacher George Wishart was burned at the stake for heresy in St Andrews. In retaliation, a Protestant mob seized St Andrews castle and murdered Cardinal Beaton, the leading ecclesiastical figure in the kingdom and a close associate of Mary of Guise. Royal forces, with French help, recaptured the castle. Among those taken was one John Knox, who was sentenced to serve two years as a galley slave in the French navy.

△ *The castle of St Andrew's*

▽ *The reformer Wishart preaching against mariolatry*

17. THE PROTESTANT TRIUMPH

In the 1540s and 1550s, Reformation ideas spread in Scotland among the same kinds of literate, urban people that had embraced them elsewhere in western Europe in the previous generation. Reform was strongest in the lowlands. Given the vigorously Catholic position of Mary of Guise, Protestantism had a disproportionate appeal to those lowland interests which disliked the overweening power of the crown. These were often the same people who remembered Flodden as a battle in which the Scots were butchered in a French cause. For such people, an English alliance had always been a possibility. Long before the Reformation, there was never any shortage of Scots noble factions prepared to truckle with the English. But now, with England turning towards Protestantism, a further shared community of interest was developing.

John Knox

The regent, meanwhile, had shipped the young queen off to France to be educated and had betrothed her to the dauphin, thus seeming to copperfasten the Auld Alliance for ever. Mary Queen of Scots married the dauphin in 1558, the same year that her staunchly Protestant cousin Elizabeth became queen of England. In 1559 John Knox returned to Scotland, toughened by exile and by years of study and ministry in Calvin's Geneva.

Knox threw all his energy and torrential eloquence behind the Lords of the Congregation, a body of militant lowlands lords devoted to radical Protestant principles and supported by English troops and cash. They were sworn enemies of Mary of Guise and of the whole French alliance, wishing to substitute an English alliance instead. Knox himself was well acquainted with England, having spent some of his years of exile there. Now he imported huge numbers of English bibles into Scotland; they proved to be an effective agent both of anglicisation

The young Mary Queen of Scots

and reform. Knox stormed through the lowlands, preaching a potent version of Calvinism and winning the allegiance of many important towns. At Perth, he interrupted a mass in the church of St John, mounted the pulpit and delivered an incendiary sermon on the evils of popery: it caused a riot which resulted in the destruction not only of St John's but also of the monasteries of Blackfriars, Greyfriars and Charterhouse in the town.

The Lords of the Congregation may have been staunch Protestants but they also had an eye to the main chance. The destruction of monasteries was not displeasing to them, since they were likely to benefit from any monastic dissolutions just as English landowners had done a generation earlier. But such acts amounted to a declaration of war on the crown and on its French patrons. A civil war

St John's Church in Perth where John Knox preached one of the most revolutionary sermons of the Scottish Reformation

threatened, with England and France involved. But then the regent, Mary of Guise, died. Both sides drew back; the French garrison returned home. What would fill the vacuum? In August 1560, the Lords of the Congregation summoned a convention – they called it a parliament, but it was not since it didn't have royal approval – and formally declared Scotland a Protestant country. They forbade the celebration of the mass on pain of imprisonment and expropriation of property for a first offence, exile for a second and death for a third. They renounced all papal claims on the country. Knox codified the revolution in the document known as the Confession of Faith.

The Reformation had triumphed. Rather like the Scottish state that the Normans had established centuries earlier, it was very much a lowland phenomenon that spread to the highlands. A small Catholic rump persisted in the highlands and islands but elsewhere the Protestant victory was complete.

18. MARY QUEEN OF SCOTS

In 1561, Mary Queen of Scots, nineteen years old and already a widow, came home to assume the crown. She was a product of the French court and a convinced Catholic. How would she rule a country that had abandoned both the French alliance and Catholicism in order to embrace a form of radical Protestantism?

She was barely installed in Edinburgh before she insisted on the celebration of mass in her private chapel at Holyrood. Knox preached against her in St Giles, thundering that one mass was more fearful in his eyes than ten thousand armed men.

The queen sent for him: she was nothing if not plucky. There followed a celebrated series of dialogues between them in which Knox did not yield an inch. The queen eventually announced that religious toleration would prevail, but all this meant in practice was that she could have her private mass. It was still outlawed everywhere else in Scotland.

The young queen's slide to disaster began in 1565 when she fell in love with Henry Stewart, Lord Darnley, son of the earl of Lennox. He was a prince of the blood and a cousin both to Mary and to Elizabeth of England. But he was a vain and vicious fop and the queen's affection for him barely survived their marriage. Darnley alienated many of the queen's advisors who inevitably saw him as an agent of the Lennox interest. Even worse, the queen soon transferred her affections to her low-born Italian secretary, David Rizzio. His influence diluted her previous policy of religious toleration and turned her towards a more aggressively Catholic course. A number of disaffected

◁ Lord Darnley

▽ This painting by Sidley (1829-96) depicts the theological debate between John Knox and Mary Queen of Scots

Castle Island in Loch Leven, where Mary Queen of Scots was held prisoner and from whence she escaped

Protestant lords led by William Ruthven and James Morton conspired with Darnley to murder Rizzio in the queen's antechamber in Holyrood in 1566. The queen, meanwhile, was pregnant and later that year she gave birth to a son, James. Relations between the queen and Darnley did not improve. Early in

> *I fear of right knowledge you have none!*
>
> John Knox
> to Mary Queen of Scots

1567 he fell ill with smallpox at Glasgow. Mary went to him, brought him back to Edinburgh and lodged him in a house at the Kirk o' Field, just outside the city walls. On the night of 9 February the house was blown up by a gunpowder explosion. Darnley died. The earl of Bothwell was tried and acquitted before a court rigged for acquittal, although it was generally believed that he was guilty and that the queen herself was complicit in her husband's murder. Bothwell was her new favourite. On 24 April, he more or less eloped with her; on 7 May he divorced his wife; on 12 May Mary made him duke of Orkney; and on 15 May she made him her husband. Darnley was barely three months dead.

It was too much. The Scots nobility and the common people alike were united in their horror of the queen's recklessness. Knox inveighed against her. Bothwell and his supporters met a superior force opposed to them at Carberry Hill near Edinburgh; they surrendered without a fight. Mary threw herself on the mercy of the rebels while Bothwell rode away and out of history.

The rebels' mercy did not amount to much. They held her prisoner first in Edinburgh where the mob, well primed by Knox's vituperations, treated her abominably. She was then taken to an island in Loch Leven and made to abdicate in favour of her son, who was crowned as James VI at Stirling on 29 July 1567. The earl of Moray was declared regent until the king was seventeen. He oversaw James' education as a Protestant, though Mary had baptised him a Catholic.

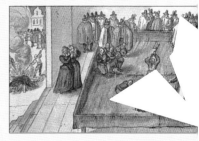

The execution of Mary Queen of Scots

Mary eventually escaped from Loch Leven in May 1568 and raised an army of 6,000 men but was easily defeated by Moray at Langside, now part of suburban Glasgow. She fled. She might have gone to France but instead she chose England, crossing the Solway Firth into the kingdom of her cousin Elizabeth and into the long limbo that preceded her execution nineteen years later.

19. THE UNION OF CROWNS

ary's infant son was now King James VI of Scotland. A series of regencies ensued until James himself took charge at the age of 17 in 1584. In general, these regencies were successful: factional struggles between the great magnate families were kept to a minimum and the country was at peace for the most part. Not that all had been smooth sailing: immediately before assuming the reins of power, the young king had been kidnapped by an ultra Protestant faction led by the earl of Gowrie in an incident known as the Raid of Ruthven. They feared the influence of the regent, the earl of Lennox who had been educated as a French Catholic and had only converted to Protestantism on his arrival in Scotland four years earlier.

The story of Scotland in the second half of the sixteenth century is dominated by the religious question. Knox, the farmer's son from Haddington in East Lothian who 'neither feared nor flattered any flesh' in the words of the regent Morton, died in 1572. He had been the key influence in the Scottish reformation. In the next generation, his place was taken by an equally fearless and unbending scholar-preacher, Andrew Melville. He was the principal author of the Second Book of Discipline, which is the real foundation text of Scots Presbyterianism and of the modern Church of Scotland.

An early Presbyterian Church

Presbyterianism is a system of church government whose roots lay in Judaism and in the primitive Christian church with its Judaic inheritance. In the Jewish tradition, synagogues and their congregations were under the direction of elected elders, the Greek word for whom was presbuteroi. However, this tradition yielded to an imperial Roman system of authority as the Christian clergy evolved in the early centuries A.D. A hierarchical structure emerged in which bishops (in Greek episkopoi, hence episcopalian) dominated. The most radical sixteenth-century reformers – Calvin and his followers in Geneva – rejected episcopacy and reverted to the purity of the original Judaic-Christian concept.

'The wisest fool in Christendom':
King James VI & I

A 19th-century painting by John Henry Lorimar entitled Ordination of Elders *accurately reflects the rigour and seriousness of Presbyterian ritual*

Melville, like Knox, had studied and ministered with Calvin in Geneva. Knox introduced the Presbyterian idea into Scotland but failed to establish it fully. Bishops of the reformed church persisted, with the power of appointment to lucrative sees in the hands of the various regents of James VI's minority. However, Melville's Second Book of Discipline of 1581 set forth the case for a pure form of Presbyterianism, in which the kirk was independent of the state. After a generation of squabbling, episcopacy was abolished under the so-called Golden Act of 1592. Presbyterianism became the normal system of governance for the Scots reformed church, although a minority of episcopal reformers still remained.

The king had acquiesced in this change only with the greatest reluctance. Indeed, he had found Melville to be as awkward and uncompromising as his mother had found Knox. James was determined that, whatever else, the kirk would not be wholly independent of the state and thus a rival centre of power and moral authority. The king was an episcopalian at heart, just as Melville was a theocrat. The uneasy, unresolved stand-off between the two was to be an echoing theme in Scottish history for centuries to come.

Then, in 1603, came one of those changes from which there is no retreat. Elizabeth of England died without an heir. James was her nearest living relative and so he now added the English throne to the Scottish. Less than a century after Flodden, the Anglo-Scots union of crowns symbolised the whole thrust of sixteenth-century Scottish history. James VI and I, the wisest fool in Christendom, left Edinburgh for the last time and rode south to London.

20. The National Covenant

James VI had been a successful king of Scotland. He had quelled the magnate factions, asserted royal authority, presided over an era of peace and reached a workable if uneasy modus vivendi with the kirk. In many ways, his success came from the effective reconciliation of opposites. In particular, the tension between his episcopalian instincts and a relentlessly Calvinist kirk obliged him to move delicately and sensitively, to trim and compromise, in short to behave politically.

to secure a union of the two parliaments. He attempted to impose uniformity in religion on both kingdoms. Naturally, given his own preferences, it was the English episcopalian model that was supposed to prevail. He overturned

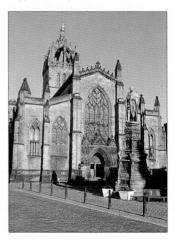

St Giles

the Golden Act of 1592 by appointing three Scottish bishops in 1610, having previously banished Andrew Melville and manipulated the general assembly of the Presbyterian Church into supporting him. By 1618 he had so thoroughly suborned the general assembly that he persuaded it to pass the notorious Five Articles of Perth, all of which were hostile to established Presbyterian practice. The fifth article, requiring that communicants should kneel to receive the sacrament, was especially offensive.

One of Van Dyck's great portraits of King Charles I

Now, at 37 years of age, he was ensconced in the more agreeable atmosphere of an Anglican kingdom. Freed of the necessity to deal directly with the fractious Scots, he allowed his autocratic and arrogant instincts to take over. He tried unsuccessfully

The articles so alienated Presbyterian opinion that they were unenforceable. Wisely, James did not press the issue. But the damage had been done. The Presbyterians, who were the preponderant element among Scots Protestants, were increasingly suspicious of royal interference in church affairs. This was to have fatal consequences for James's successor, Charles I.

Charles succeeded on the death of his father in 1625. His French queen, Henrietta Maria, held views on kingship that had been formed in Paris. She favoured the divine right theory of autocratic kingship; she was also a Roman Catholic. Charles was an Anglican, but of such a kind that he was widely suspected of sharing his wife's religious sympathies.

> *'The Church is an anvil which has worn out many hammers', and the story of the first collision is, in essentials, the story of all.*
>
> Alexander Maclaren

Charles had been born in Scotland but had not been there since he was four, cared little for it and understood less. He did not bother to visit the country until 1633 for his formal coronation as king of Scotland. His visit was a disaster. He restored the kirk of St Giles to cathedral status, appointed a bishop to it, had himself anointed with oil, reintroduced the surplice as an item of priestly attire and was openly accompanied by Archbishop Laud of Canterbury who was widely believed to be trying to effect a Roman Catholic revival in England!

It got worse. In the following years, he tried to introduce a new Book of Common Prayer as revised by Laud and by the Scottish bishops. Presbyterians had rejected the older common prayer book in favour of Knox's Book of Common Order, so this new imposition was doubly hateful in their eyes. Its first attempted use in St Giles in 1637 produced a riot.

The result was the great National Covenant of 1638. The idea of a special covenant between God and his chosen people was originally a Jewish idea which was revived by Calvinists. There had been covenants – declarations or petitions – before but nothing on the scale of what now happened. Over 300,000 Scots signed the Covenant, "a glorious marriage of the kingdom with God". Presbyterianism declared itself a national church, in fact if not in law. It declared itself independent of the king and the state. The question that James VI and Andrew Melville had fudged forty years earlier could be fudged no longer. Presbyterian Scotland was in open revolt.

Queen Henrietta Maria

21. CIVIL WAR

APresbyterian general assembly in Glasgow duly rejected the Prayer Book and abolished the bishoprics. Charles I might well have echoed his father's aphorism "no bishop, no king". At any rate, he rejected the assembly's decisions.

Charles was trapped between the Scots Presbyterians and the English parliamentarians. He opted to buy off the former, visiting Edinburgh in 1641. He confirmed the Presbyterian nature of the kirk and undertook that all future Scottish government appointments would be made only with the advice and consent of the Scots parliament. Thus he conceded parliamentary government in Scotland just as he prepared to resist it in England.

Civil war broke out in England between king and parliament. The Scots, although naturally sympathetic to parliament, tried not to take sides lest they jeopardise the Presbyterian triumph so recently secured. But this proved impossible, if only because both sides in England sought Scottish help. Both sides got it.

The principal alliance was that between the Covenanters and the parliamentarians. The Covenanters

Alexander Leslie, First Earl of Leven, the brilliant leader of the Covenanter Army

The Covenanters raised an army under Alexander Leslie, a veteran of the Thirty Years War in which he had fought for the Swedes. An inadequate royal force marched north, only to meet humiliation at the hands of Leslie's army. The Scots ravaged Northumberland and Durham and occupied Newcastle-upon-Tyne. The king had to recall the English parliament to vote supplies for a proper royal army, thus ending eleven years of personal, non-parliamentary rule. Naturally, parliament wanted guarantees that the king would cease his practice of arbitrary rule.

James Graham, Marquis of Montrose

Cromwell at Marston Moor, a painting by Ernest Crofts (1847-1911)

feared a royal victory in England which might presage an undoing of the 1641 settlement in Scotland. Moreover, they saw a chance to establish Presbyterianism throughout Britain and made an agreement with the English parliamentarians to that end in the Solemn League and Covenant of 1643.

However, some Scots were appalled at this open rebellion against their lawful king. The leader of this faction was James Graham, earl of Montrose. He had been one of the four original drafters of the National Covenant but he recoiled from extremist Presbyterianism and was impressed by the king's concessions in 1641. In 1644 he was appointed royal lieutenant in Scotland and he quickly raised a highland army which won six battles that year. He skillfully exploited ancient clan hatreds, especially those between the Campbells of Argyll and the MacDonalds of the Isles which went back centuries. But when he tried to break into the Presbyterian stronghold in the lowlands he was defeated at Philiphaugh in 1645.

Meanwhile Leslie had taken a Scottish army of 25,000 men south to fight alongside the English parliamentary forces under Fairfax and Cromwell. They contributed to the decisive victories at Marston Moor (1644) and Naseby (1645). But the English parliamentarians could not deliver on their bargain with the Scots. Power had now effectively passed to the military wing, which contained a strong Independent influence. Although Calvinist, the English Independents favoured a decentralised church structure; they disliked the Scots Presbyterian model, with its authoritarian aspects. Cromwell was the dominant Independent.

The Scots felt betrayed. Then, in

Philiphaugh, where Montrose was defeated in 1645

May 1646, the king suddenly surrendered to their army in the English midlands. He hoped to come to an agreement with the Scots which would divide them from the parliamentarians. The Scots price was a promise to establish Presbyterianism in England. Charles refused. The Scots handed him over to the English, who promptly imprisoned him.

22. CROMWELL AND CHARLES II

King Charles I was executed in Whitehall on 30 January 1649. The news came like a thunderclap in Scotland. For all his faults, he had been their lawful king and now he had been put to death by foreigners. The Scottish government, by now in the hands of a landed oligarchy under Archibald Campbell, 8th earl of Argyll, promptly declared the dead king's son as Charles II of Scotland. Under duress, the new king accepted the Covenant although he had no intention of honouring this promise: for him, famously, Presbyterianism was "not a religion for gentlemen".

Cromwell

The proclamation of the king in Scotland meant that Cromwell was almost certain to invade. This he did, demanding that the Scots hand over the son as they had done the father. He crushed the Scots at the battle of Dunbar, occupied Edinburgh and reduced the lowlands. Charles went north across the Forth where he was crowned at Scone on 1 January 1651. In a last throw, the Scots now invaded England only to meet final

The execution of Charles I outside the Palace of Whitehall in London, January 1649

defeat at Worcester on 3 September 1651. The king fled abroad.

Cromwell was the undisputed master of England and Scotland alike. Scots independence was snuffed out. Yet the Cromwellian years at least brought peace and stability. Law and order was enforced by the Lord Protector's troops and religious toleration observed. But Cromwell's regime barely survived Cromwell, whose death in 1658 was followed two years later by the restoration of Charles II in both kingdoms.

Charles promptly reneged on all his promises to the Scots. He restored episcopacy; he never again set foot in his northern kingdom whose parliament he blithely ignored; he ran its affairs through a revived privy council based in London. The dominant figure in the Scottish administration for most of Charles II's reign was John Maitland, Earl of Lauderdale.

The restoration of episcopacy and the appointment of bishops led to Presbyterian disaffection and revolt. This was especially severe in the south-west lowlands, in southern Argyll and Galloway – an area that thus maintained its ancient habit of awkward particularism. The government then made attendance at Sunday service under the

A.C. Gow's 19th-century painting of Cromwell at the battle of Dunbar

episcopal rite compulsory. To no avail. The western Covenanters met illegally in what became known as conventicles and even briefly rose in a revolt that was quickly and savagely crushed.

At this point, the distinction between Covenanters and mainstream Presbyterianism begins to emerge more clearly. The former was more extreme and generally more rural and remote. The latter, while still utterly refusing to conform to episcopal

orthodoxy, was more temperate, as befitted a movement whose principal adherents were educated urban people. In part, the division was regional.

In 1679, a party of Covenanting zealots murdered James Sharp, the archbishop of St Andrews. The murderers escaped to the west, joining up with their disaffected brethren there and touching off a full-scale rebellion that ended in defeat at the battle of Bothwell Bridge.

In effect, Lauderdale had tried to ram episcopacy down the throats of the Scots who simply refused to have it. True, there was a traditional centre of episcopal allegiance in the north-east. There were even residual Roman Catholic communities in the highlands and islands, as there still are today. And, as we have seen, Presbyterianism itself was fissile. Yet the fact remains that Calvinism was the choice of a great majority of Scots, especially in the lowlands, and this choice was an expression of Scottish independence. The lowland Scots would not conform to the state religion, as was the European norm. At some point or other, this highly unusual state of affairs had to be resolved. The resolution was nearer than anyone hoped or feared.

Ardchattan Priory near Oban. This priory which dated from the 13th century was burned by Cromwell's troops in 1654

23. PRESBYTERIAN TRIUMPH

Lauderdale was replaced as royal commissioner for Scotland by none other than the king's brother, James Stewart, a Roman Catholic. He persisted in Lauderdale's policy of attempting a restoration of episcopacy. Indeed, he intensified it. The Test Act of 1681 was a deliberate attempt to establish royal control over the Scottish church by obliging all office holders, either in church or state, to swear an oath abjuring the Covenant.

This led to the period known in Scottish history as the killing time. There was a wholesale persecution of Presbyterians for most of the 1680s, as the crown attempted to extirpate Calvinism. Although cruel, the persecution was not mindless. All over Europe, religious minorities were treated roughly and made to conform to the state religion; otherwise they were regarded as traitors to the state and possible

King William II & III. This portrait is attributed to Kneller

agents of foreign powers. Religious conformity was a tried and trusted formula for keeping domestic peace. The Scots were out of line. Moreover, they were divided: there were regional differences within Calvinism and even regions where episcopacy and Roman Catholicism had support. So James's persecution, while seeming doomed, futile and heartless to us, would not have seemed so to contemporaries.

James succeeded his brother on the throne in 1685 as James VII (II of England) and overplayed his hand by adopting a policy of almost total religious toleration. Although designed principally to help his fellow Roman Catholics – less than a decade after the notorious Popish Plot – it also gave relief to such groups as the Quakers. From a twentieth-century perspective, it might appear to be a model of liberalism. Given the realities of seventeenth-century power, it

King James VII & II

offended too many important interest groups in England and Scotland alike.

Then in 1688 the queen, after six fruitless pregnancies, gave birth to a son and ensured the Catholic succession in both kingdoms. It was too much. English Protestants offered the throne to William of Orange who was married to James's daughter Mary. He was a Calvinist. He landed at Torbay in Devon on 5 November 1688. After much prevarication, James fled. It was a successful coup d'etat and therefore acquired a grandiose title: the Glorious Revolution.

Viscount Dundee, the leader of Episcopalian revolt in the north east

Into the resulting vacuum in Scotland flowed a self-constituted body of lowland grandees, Presbyterian to a man, who promptly declared James to have forfeited the throne which they offered instead to William, subject to his promising to abolish episcopacy. He accepted.

Not all Scots were happy with this demarche. A brief rebellion under the royalist Lord Dundee drew support from the episcopalian north-east and the highlands, where Dundee raised an army. After a victory at Killiecrankie in which Dundee died, the rebellion petered out. It was an old theme in Scottish history: the big decisions were made in the lowlands and imposed, if needs be, on the rest of the country.

A modern view of Killiecranke, site of the crucial battle of 1689

The Revolution settlement established Presbyterianism as the state church in Scotland, thus recognising in the most obvious way the depth of Scottish particularism. It was and is the only established church anywhere in the Christian world which is not organised on the episcopal principle. The kirk was not generous in its hour of triumph. Within ten years, almost two-thirds of all ministers had been forced out of their cures by orthodox Presbyterians. These included every range of opinion from episcopalians to radical Covenanters who objected to William II as an uncovenanted king, underlining yet again the determination of the newly ascendant kirk to assert its uniform authority throughout a varied land. In the 1690s, lowlands Presbyterianism was a classic beggar on horseback.

24. GLENCOE

The massacre of Glencoe in 1692 is one of the most notorious events in Scottish history. In the aftermath of the Revolution settlement, the highlands were still restless and a potential threat to the survival of the new regime. In order to command the allegiance of the clan chiefs, all were required to sign an oath of loyalty to King William II by 1 January 1692. The logic was the same as that of the Test Act of 1681, but directed by those who had been the victims of that act against groups which they feared were now a threat to their newly established position.

The penalties for those who failed or refused to swear the oath were ferocious: their lands would be forfeit; their homes open to destruction; they and their families would be outlawed and might be murdered at will. Most chiefs signed by the appointed date. One who did not was Maclan of Glencoe, the elderly head of a cadet branch of the MacDonalds. He first went to the wrong place to swear the oath and then had to make a frightful mid-winter journey from Glencoe, just south of Ben Nevis, to Inveraray near the head of Lough Fyne, a distance of forty miles. He eventually arrived and swore the oath but his lateness in doing so offered a pretext to those in Edinburgh who favoured rough measures in the highlands.

The villain of the piece was John Dalrymple of Stair, secretary of state for Scotland. He devised the scheme

△ A 19th-century reconstruction of the death of Maclan at Glencoe

▽ The pass of Glencoe in winter

A detail from J. B. MacDonald's romantic image of the Glencoe massacre

and secured the king's signature for it. What ensued was not an accident, or something that was relatively innocent in intention but which got out of hand. The massacre was planned. There was to be no mercy.

The MacDonalds of Glencoe were believed to be Roman Catholic. They were also wild, lawless upland people. On 1 February 1692, troops were quartered in the glen ostensibly for non-payment of taxes. And not just any troops: they were the earl of Argyll's regiment. The earls of Argyll were Campbells, the hereditary enemies of the MacDonalds for centuries. The officer commanding

was Captain Robert Campbell of Glenlyon. He dined with MacIan on the night of 5 February. At first light the following morning, his men fell upon the unsuspecting MacDonalds and slaughtered thirty-eight of them, a less than satisfactory result in that their orders had been to butcher everyone under seventy years old.

Glencoe was a government-sponsored massacre. The troops used may have been Campbells but they were regulars under proper military command, carrying out a national policy. It was this government complicity that made Glencoe so notorious. It speaks volumes for the rancour and division within Scotland that such an act could be orchestrated in this way. The lowland Presbyterian triumph, which at first glance might seem absolute, was by no means so. It was vulnerable – or felt itself vulnerable – to that more traditional, clan-based society that still dominated the highlands. Presbyterian hegemony was most assured south of the Forth-Clyde line, which was still as significant a cultural dividing line as it had been in Roman times.

25. The Act of Union

The possibility of a union between England and Scotland had been implicit in all of Scots history since the Reformation. Why it did not happen sooner was simple. It was massively unpopular with a majority of Scots. Popular anglophobia was never far beneath the surface, and these were stressful times. For example, the English parliament passed the Act of Settlement of 1701 without any reference to the Scottish parliament: it blithely arranged for the royal succession in both kingdoms. The English Navigation Acts severely damaged Scottish trade. The English went to war with France in 1701 without consulting the Scottish parliament, although this meant deploying Scottish regiments.

None the less, there were other forces at work as well. First there was the mutual fear of Catholic France and anxiety about French support for highland Jacobites – as the supporters of James VII and his successors were called (from Jacobus, the Latin word for James).

A view of the old Scottish Parliament

The traditional alliance between Scottish Calvinism and England had been deepened by the nature of the revolution settlement which established Presbyterianism.

Then there was the trauma of the Darien Venture, in which thousands

James Ogilvie, first Earl of Seafield and Chancellor of Scotland at the time of the Act of Union

of Scots investors lost fortunes in a harebrained scheme to colonise Panama using the example of the massively profitable East India Company as a guide. The whole

scheme collapsed in 1700, convincing many Scots that they could not prosper in international trade without the access to imperial markets which a union would give them. A go-it-alone commercial policy seemed doomed, especially with the obstacles which the Navigation Acts presented. There was also the brutal reality that in 1700 England took half of all Scotland's exports.

Under the English Act of Settlement William of Orange was succeeded by Anne, a Protestant and the last surviving daughter of James VII. But she was childless and the old king – her father – had a son whom the Catholic powers of Europe recognised as the legitimate heir to the English and Scottish thrones. In order that his claim should be frustrated, the London parliament decided that Queen Anne should be succeeded by a Protestant: her nearest Protestant relations were the children of Sophia, Electress of Hanover, a granddaughter of James VI and I. Thus the act secured the Hanoverian succession over the more legitimate claims of the Catholic Stewarts.

The lowland Scots liked the act but not its implicit claim to bind Scotland. The Edinburgh parliament passed an Act of Security, reserving its own right to legislate for the Scottish succession. For good measure, it passed another act "Anent Peace and War" which did the same for military affairs. London was enraged and retaliated with an Aliens Act which put it up to the Scots either to

Queen Anne

repeal the Act of Security or else enter into talks for a union. Otherwise crippling trade sanctions would be imposed.

The Scots went into an anti-English frenzy over this threat but the crisis at least brought everything to a head. It also concentrated minds, especially among those Scots who felt that a union was Scotland's best long-term option. The basic problem was how to protect Scottish particularism – her profound sense of being a separate nation – from English dominance. It is fair to say that the pro-union Scots were a lowland minority, driven by a clear-headed understanding of economic necessity (both Scotland's and their own) who railroaded the proposal through. In the end, the union of 1707 guaranteed the independence of the Church of Scotland and left the legal and education systems alone. A British free trade area was created. But Scotland lost her sovereignty, her parliament and her coinage. She was still a nation, but suddenly a nation without a state.

There's an end to an auld sang.

Lord Seafield, the Chancellor, announcing the parliamentary vote for union.

---

26. THE '15

By the early eighteenth century, all the recognisable elements of modern Scotland were in place. The country was united with England in the new state known as Great Britain. The Hanoverian succession was a fact: the Stewarts were finished. The established Church of Scotland was Presbyterian.

This is the Scotland we know and take for granted. But for contemporaries, these arrangements were not only new; they were potentially reversible. Significant numbers of Scots resented the union, a situation that persists to this day. Many regarded the Hanoverians as foreign usurpers. By any reckoning they had a good point: the Stewarts had a far better title to the thrones of both kingdoms than the Hanoverians but had been cast aside out of political necessity or convenience, depending on one's point of view.

△ *The Earl of Mar raises the Jacobite standard in 1715. This is a 19th-century representation*

The Scottish Jacobites wished to see a restoration of the Stewarts. Some were simply legitimists who believed in the sanctity of lawful kingship; some were nationalists who wanted a Scots rather than a

---

There's some say that we wan,
some say that they wan,
Some say that nane
wan at a', man;
But one thing I'm sure,
that at Sheriffmuir
A battle there was which
I saw, man:
And we ran, and they ran, and
they ran, and we ran,
And we ran; and they ran
awa', man!

Murdoch McLennan

German dynasty; some were regional protest groups like the highland Catholics or the Moray episcopalians, chafing under the importunities of the kirk. These categories often overlapped but they all added up to a potential threat to the new arrangements. Twice in the first half of the eighteenth century, in 1715 and in 1745, there were serious rebellions. It is important to remember that these were rebellions

▽ *King George I, who founded the Hanoverian dynasty*

Another 19th-century painting which reconstructs the battle of Sheriffmuir in 1715

The '15 was a serious threat to the revolution settlement. Mar's incompetence concealed the danger. The leader of the crown forces, the 2nd duke of Argyll, reckoned that nine out of ten Scots supported the rebellion, almost certainly an exaggeration but suggestive none the less. A more decisive campaign might have made common cause with English Jacobites and might have had French military support.

Kildrummy Castle, ten miles west of Alford, dated from 13th century and was the seat of the Earl of Mar. It was destroyed after the failed rising of 1715.

not just against London but against the new regime in Edinburgh as well. London and Edinburgh were now hand in glove.

James VII had died in exile in 1701. His son, known to history as the Old Pretender, was recognised by the Scots Jacobites as James VIII. In 1715, the Hanoverian George I ascended the throne. The episcopalians of the north-east rose and proclaimed King James VIII. Making common cause with some of the highland clans, an army was formed under the leadership of the earl of Mar, a man who proved spectacularly unfit for leadership. Despite outnumbering the crown forces sent against him by more than two-to-one, he still managed to lose the decisive battle of Sheriffmuir. He failed to co-ordinate his actions or otherwise link up with restless English Jacobites. In all, his rebellion was over even before the Old Pretender arrived at Peterhead just before Christmas. James stayed in Scotland for a few weeks before slipping back to France. He never returned.

But here was a telling point. James, "The Old Pretender", was a Catholic who showed no inclination to change his religion, even to episcopalianism. The forces aligned in Scotland in 1715 were strikingly similar to those in 1560. The lowland Calvinists were firm for the English alliance as their best protection: that alliance was now formalised in the union. They were, when all was said and done, the heart of the nation. Too much had happened in Scotland in a century and a half for a French-supported Catholic ever to regain the throne without setting off a civil war. The revolution settlement was still a bit shaky but it had survived its first big test. There was just one more to come.

27. BONNIE PRINCE CHARLIE

Charles Edward Stewart was the son of the Old Pretender. In July 1745 he landed in the Outer Hebrides, raised a highland army, proclaimed his father king just as Mar had done thirty years earlier and swept through Scotland. He was young, handsome and brave – the very stuff of romance. And although his adventure ended in tragedy and farce, that aura of romance surrounded him to the end.

Bonnie Prince Charlie

Scots Highland soldiers from a print of 1786

The '45 should never have happened. There was no French support. An invasion planned for the previous year had been abandoned. The revolution settlement had taken further root. Yet the young prince took Scotland by storm. Within two months of his landing, he had swept out of his highland base, trounced the government army at Prestonpans and occupied the city of Edinburgh, although not the castle. Together with a number of highland forts, it never fell to the prince. But the rest of Scotland did.

By 4 December he had reached as far south as Derby, only 130 miles from London. He was, after all, trying to establish his family's claim to the throne of both kingdoms. His army of highlanders numbered no more than 5,000 and on their march south they had attracted hardly any additional support. Most of the British army, which numbered 62,000 in all, was on the continent fighting the French. But gradually the London government began to mobilise its forces and the Jacobite generals bowed to the inevitable. They turned back at Derby. How could they possibly hope to capture and hold a whole kingdom with a mere 5,000 men?

It was not just in England that the prince lacked popular support. In all the lowland towns and cities that he occupied, he imposed military governors rather than hold new burgh elections. Presbyterian clergy preached loyalist sermons even while under occupation. The Jacobite governors of Dundee and Perth were attacked by pro-Hanoverian mobs on 30 October, King George II's birthday. Nowhere in the lowlands was there any popular enthusiasm for Charles.

Naturally, he withdrew to his highland base. Already his army was suffering desertions: it was clear that the game was up. The grim finale came on 16 April 1746 at Culloden Moor near Inverness when government troops under the king's second son William, Duke of Cumberland, cut down the highlanders in the last pitched battle fought on British soil. The prince slipped away, thus saving his own skin but leaving the clansmen to the vengeance of the swinish Cumberland. There followed a brutal reduction of the highland clans: the chiefs were stripped of all their traditional powers; cottages were burned; people were jailed and transported; crops and stock were appropriated. It was a wholesale assault on an immemorial way of life. Nowhere was this assault more warmly applauded than in the lowland towns.

Charles Edward Stewart was hunted through the highlands and islands by Cumberland's troops but to no avail. He finally slipped away, disguised as Betty Burke – an Irish servant – under the protection of the heroic Flora MacDonald in whose boat he was rowed across to Skye. From there he escaped to France. He lived for another forty-three useless years, a squalid alcoholic who never ceased to berate the highlanders whom he had abandoned so blithely and who had suffered so horribly in his cause.

△ Flora MacDonald

▽ A contemporary view of the Duke of Cumberland at the Battle of Culloden

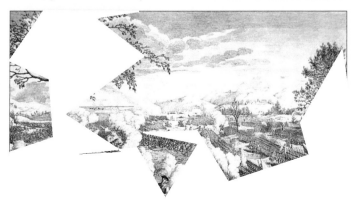

28. Scottish Enlightenment

The victory at Culloden finally secured the revolution settlement and completed the triumph of the lowlands over the highlands. The Old Pretender died in 1766, whereupon the Pope declined to recognise Charles Edward Stewart as king. Instead he acknowledged reality.

There followed that outburst of creative energy in the lowlands, born of the security of victory, known as the Scottish Enlightenment. It was centred on Edinburgh, which supported an astonishing variety of learned and scientific societies throughout the eighteenth century. They all contributed to the exceptional intellectual life that characterised the Scottish capital. Europe had many regional capitals distinguished for the vitality of their social and intellectual life but even contemporaries acknowledged the primacy of Edinburgh.

Exactly why this was is a matter of dispute but a number of points can be made. First, the lowland tradition of literacy flowed from the need of a Protestant people to be able to read the Bible. Second, the country could boast four ancient universities of real distinction: St Andrews (founded 1412), Glasgow (1451), Aberdeen (1495) and Edinburgh (1583). Third, eighteenth-century Scotland supported a cultivated aristocracy and middle class: its separate systems in church, law and education provided a domestic focus for their energies. There was no wholesale flight of talent to England and overseas until the nineteenth century.

△ *Edinburgh Rock and Castle*

▽ *Robert Burns at a fashionable literary salon at Edinburgh*

In addition to all that, Scotland was simply lucky. For any small country to have produced such utterly brilliant figures as David Hume, Robert Adam, Thomas Telford, James Boswell, Robert Burns, Adam Smith, James Watt and Walter Scott within a couple of generations suggests a certain good fortune. Each was a person of world stature in his field, but in addition there was a host of other outstanding talents. The lawyer Francis Jeffrey founded the *Edinburgh Review* in 1802, one of the most influential of all journals in nineteenth-century Britain. Allan Ramsay (1684-1758) was an editor and poet of genuine stature and the most important literary figure in the generation before Burns. Even the tragi-comic figure of James Macpherson, the fraud who claimed to have translated the ancient Celtic poet Ossian (most of the work was his own invention) was part of this frenetically energetic milieu.

The most visible evidence of the Scottish Enlightenment was the building of Edinburgh New Town, begun in 1767 to the plan of the architect James Craig. The Nor' Loch, a swamp that lay to the north of the medieval city, was drained and built on. The New Town is the biggest and most coherent Georgian estate in the world. In its severe beauty, there is nothing like it anywhere. As in Dublin and Bath, it takes the elements of the international Georgian style and adapts them uniquely to the imperatives of local landscape and stone. The result is a treasure of architectural coherence.

It is also a statement of Scotland's new position in the world in the second half of the eighteenth century. The new town was built to house the Scottish elite, whose world was still firmly focused on Edinburgh. Yet the style it adopted was international and cosmopolitan, with local variations. Rather like Hungary within the Habsburg empire, Scotland retained its highly articulated personality within a larger entity.

Charlotte Square in Edinburgh

But that larger entity was central to its fortunes. The lowland-English alliance that eventually produced the Act of Union also gave Edinburgh New Town its nomenclature. Princes Street is named for the sons of King George III; Queen Street and Charlotte Square for his wife; George Street for the king himself. Hanover Street is named for the dynasty that some Scots accepted only with misgivings but whose legitimacy the lowlanders never really questioned when it came to the crunch.

29. THE CLEARANCES

The destruction of the highland clan system followed the defeat at Culloden. Many clan chiefs were exiled, others expropriated. The ancient clan-based system of landholding, in which land was regarded as a communal resource held in trust by the chief for his people and their descendants, suffered a frontal attack. But lowland law did not recognise such a system of landholding. It treated chiefs as landowners pure and simple.

Strathnaver, site of some of the most notorious clearances

The half-century after Culloden was also the age of agricultural improvement. New theories of capitalist farming became fashionable, putting the emphasis on more efficient use of land, on increased crop yields, on modern methods of cultivation and fertilisation. The land was seen as a resource to be exploited, not as an inheritance to be preserved.

This dynamic view of landholding demanded the energies of individual landowners and their managers to make it work. It was obviously incompatible with the older clan view of land. With the end of the clan system, however, a perfect opportunity arose to test the new theories. It was not only new lowland or English owners who embraced them. Many surviving chiefs recognised that the old game was up, that a way of life that had survived from time immemorial was now gone for good; now they too began to behave like the individual landowners that the law said they were.

The highland clearances aimed to move the surplus population off the land to facilitate its efficient economic exploitation. There were two forms of displacement. One involved the movement of tenants from the inland to the coastal parts of large estates in order to clear the straths, the rich river valleys which contained nearly all the good land in the highlands. Under the clans, the straths had been used for tillage to provide food. Now they were turned over to sheep, as were vast areas of the highlands. Of all the various types of new agriculture tried in the late eighteenth century, sheep farming proved to be the most profitable. But it was only profitable when conducted on a large scale. And it required very little human labour. That meant displacing a lot of people for a lot of sheep.

The black-faced sheep which replaced the evicted highland crofters

The second form of clearance was simple migration to the booming economy of the lowlands where the industrial revolution was beginning to bite, or actual emigration overseas. Many emigrants went voluntarily, taking advantage of assisted emigration schemes which were funded by landowners. But many others were forced out.

The most famous clearances were on the vast estates of Elizabeth, Countess of Sutherland. She prosecuted the clearance policy with a cruel thoroughness that was matched by her notorious factor or agent, Patrick Sellar. In Strathnaver, Sellar expelled all his tenants on the right bank of the River Naver and burnt their houses. In the Strath of Kildonan, the countess pursued a similar policy to such effect that between 1811 and 1831 the population fell from 1,574 to 257.

It was this kind of heartless greed that fired the folk memories of the clearances. The fact that the landowners were often alien in blood and religion – whether they were of lowland or English stock – did not help, although the greatest resentment was reserved for those clan chiefs turned new-style landowners. They were perceived to have betrayed an ancient trust.

Loch Hope and Ben Arkle in Sutherland is a typical post-clearance highland landscape

The net effect of the clearances was to depopulate the inland parts of the highlands and turn them into enormous sheep runs. Between 1780 and 1850, the period of the principal clearances, highlanders were displaced to the coasts and the islands, or to the industrialising lowlands, or overseas. It was the final destruction of a communal way of life that could be traced back to the Picts.

Dunrobin, the seat of the Countess of Sutherland

30. INDUSTRIAL REVOLUTION

The industrial revolution was the product of technological development. First, traditional crafts such as spinning and weaving were mechanised, creating the basis of the modern textile industry. Second, James Watt developed an efficient steam engine in the 1780s, providing a source of power that could be harnessed to mass production. Third, the development of the factory system centralised production and led to the rise of industrial towns.

△ *The Lanarkshire coalfields*

▽ *James Watt, the great engineer*

Lowland Scotland had the huge advantage of abundant reserves of coal and iron. These were concentrated in the south-west and their importance in early industrial development accounts for the phenomenal rise of Glasgow as one of the great British cities of the nineteenth century.

The Lanarkshire coalfields were the richest and most productive of all Scottish fields. Overall, the Scottish mining industry grew and grew throughout the nineteenth century, producing over 40 million tons of coal on the eve of the Great War and employing over 150,000 men.

Coal and iron were intimately linked, one providing the energy source for the blast furnaces that produced the other. Great iron and coal dynasties developed, as entrepreneurs attempted to control and harness whole areas of industrial development. The main Scottish concentration was on pig iron, the most basic product of the furnaces. The iron masters were reluctant to develop into the refining processes

The Lanarkshire shipyard on the Clyde

that produced the much tougher wrought iron and later steel. In the long run, this proved to be a weakness but for three generations Scotland was one of the world's leading producers of pig iron, most of it for export.

> *There are few more impressive sights in the world than a Scotsman on the make.*
>
> **Sir James Barrie**

The presence of iron and coal facilitated the development of the third great Scottish industrial enterprise, shipbuilding. A country with such an indented coastline and one whose history was so influenced by the sea was bound to have a tradition of shipbuilding. This tradition expanded in the nineteenth century into one of the world's great industrial enterprises. The Clyde shipyards pioneered the building of iron ships in the 1840s and throughout the century they stayed in the forefront of marine engineering developments.

The manner in which shipbuilding developed can be traced in the story of one company. David Napier, a celebrated engineer, had first made his name in the 1820s. He opened his own shipyard at Govan in 1841. Among his most brilliant employees were the brothers James and George Thomson who set up in business for themselves at Finnieston in 1847. In 1899, Thomsons' was bought by the Sheffield steelmaker John Brown. Eight years later, Browns' bought a half-interest in the Harland & Wolff yard in Belfast to create the biggest shipbuilders in the world. It was barely eighty years since Napier first made his reputation.

The Gorbals, Glasgow's most notorious slum

This welter of industrial expansion sucked in labour from the countryside, the highlands and Ireland. In the case of the Catholic Irish, by the late nineteenth century a numerous minority in the Glasgow area, it gave rise to quite vicious sectarian rivalries which persist to the present day in the poisoned atmosphere of Rangers-Celtic football matches. It also produced horrific living conditions for the very poor, symbolised by the Gorbals, Glasgow's most notorious slum area – a sink of human heroism and misery that had few parallels anywhere in the developed world.

31. THE TWENTIETH CENTURY

During the latter part of the nineteenth century, Scotland generally sent a majority of Liberal MPs to Westminster, a pattern that peaked in the landslide election of 1906 when the Liberals won 58 per cent of the total vote in Scotland. But thereafter, in Scotland as in the rest of Britain, Labour gradually displaced the Liberals as the main anti-Conservative force in politics.

The industrial revolution created a huge working class population in Scotland. In 1888, James Keir Hardie (1856-1915) founded the Scottish Labour Party. It later became part of the Independent Labour party, founded in Sheffield in 1893 with Keir Hardie as its first leader. By now he was an MP, having been elected for a London constituency the previous year. In 1906, the Labour Party itself was formed, once more under

Keir Hardie

Hardie's leadership. In 1911, he was succeeded by James Ramsay MacDonald, another Scot, who in 1924 became the first Labour prime minister of the United Kingdom.

The Labour advance in Scotland was most marked in the wake of the Great War. In the 1922 general election, ten of the fifteen Glasgow seats went to the party. The city had traditionally been Liberal, but radical trade unionism and Marxist politics made the city a centre of left-wing activity. The activities of the Red Clydesiders in the years 1915-22 – organisers and orators such as John Maclean, William Gallacher and James Maxton – terrified the more respectable elements in Scottish life with the spectre of revolution. The weight of working-class numbers was made to tell. A hastily-called general strike threatened to bring the city to its knees in early 1919 until broken by police brutality, troops and tanks.

Ramsay MacDonald

This was the high-water mark of naive or heroic socialist agitation, depending on one's point of view. Thereafter, Labour was the principal anti-Tory force in Scotland but as late as 1955 the Conservatives were still the largest single party in the country in terms of parliamentary seats. Interestingly the Tories' heartland was in the north-east, where the old episcopalian tradition still lived on. Since then, Labour has dominated Scottish politics.

The discovery of oil and gas off the Scottish coast has transformed the onshore economy

Labour's national reliance on Scotland – as on Wales and the north of England – for possible national majorities lies behind its occasional confusion of the question of Scottish nationalist aspirations. For many years, the party was in favour of Scottish home rule. It dropped this policy in 1958. Into the resulting vacuum moved a revived Scottish National Party, campaigning for full independence. It had a number of spectacular by-election successes at Labour's expense in the late '60s and '70s and it eventually forced a reluctant Westminster to propose a devolution referendum in 1979. Labour, which rightly feared the potential of the SNP, inserted a clause in the enabling legislation which meant that a simple majority would not suffice; 40 per cent of the total electorate would have to support the measure. It got the simple majority but not the 40 per cent. Shortly after, Margaret Thatcher came to power, making the question academic.

It remained so until Labour's landslide victory of May 1997. Four out of five Scots voted for some form of constitutional change. The Conservatives were wiped out in Scotland, despite winning eighteen per cent of the vote. The SNP returned six MPs on a platform of full independence. Labour, with 56 Scottish seats and huge national majority, took office in London and appointed Donald Dewar as Scottish Secretary to deliver on their promise of a devolved assembly. Exactly what form it will take is uncertain at the time of writing. But some form of devolution is clearly being demanded by the Scots. As the twentieth century ends, Scotland's relationship with the rest of Britain is once more the paramount question. It was ever thus.

A poster for the Scottish National Party

INDEX

ACKNOWLEDGEMENTS

AKG LONDON
p 38 (top)

ART AND ARCHITECTURE COLLECTION, PINNER
pp 12 (centre), 14, 17 (bot), 20 (top), 21, 28 (bot)

BRIDGEMAN ART LIBRARY, LONDON
pp 28 (top) British Library, 32 (bot) British Library, 33 National
Library of Scotland, Edinburgh, 42 (bot) Towneley Hall Art Gallery, 57
Blenheim Palace, Oxon

CLAUDE POULET © CLB INTERNATIONAL
cover: sporran and pp 1, 2, 4

DENNIS HARDLEY PHOTOGRAPHY, OBAN
pp 12 (bot and cover), 18 (bot), 37 (top) 39 (top)

HISTORIC SCOTLAND © CROWN COPYRIGHT RESERVED
pp 11 (top), 13 (top), 23, 24, 43 (top), 51 (bot)

NATIONAL MUSEUM OF SCOTLAND, EDINBURGH
pp 66 (top), 67 (bot)

NATIONAL PORTRAIT GALLERY OF SCOTLAND, EDINBURGH
pp 16 (top), 18 (top), 31 (bot), 34 (top), 35 (top), 36 (top), 38 (bot),
39 (bot), 40 and on cover, 42 (top), 43 (bot), 44 (bot), 45, 47, 48,
50 (bot), 52, 53 (left), 54 (top), 55, 56 (top), 58 (right), 61 (top),
62 (bot), 63 (top), 66 (bot), 68

PETER NEWARK'S PICTURES, BATH
pp 15 (top), 25 (bot), 29 (top), 32 (top), 37 (bot), 49 (top), 51 (top),
54 (top), 55 (top), 58 (left), 59 (top), 60 (bot), 61 (bot)

SCOTLAND IN FOCUS, GALASHIELS
pp 8, 9, 10, 11 (bot), 13 (bot), 15 (bot), 16 (bot), 17 (top), 19,
20 (bot), 22, 25 (top), 26, 27, 29 (bot), 30 and on cover, 31 (top),
34 (bot), 35 (bot), 36 (bot), 41, 44 (top), 46 (right), 49 (bot),
53 (right), 54 (bot), 56 (bot), 59 (bot), 60 (top and on cover),
63 (bot), 64, 65, 67 (top), 69 (top), and cover: stained glass window
of William Wallace, Edinburgh at night, the Forth Bridge

SCOTTISH NATIONAL PARTY, EDINBURGH
p 69 (bot)

SOTHEBYS TRANSPARENCY LIBRARY, LONDON
pp 46 (left), 50 (top)